The Quality Interview

Getting It Right on Both Sides of the Mic

The Quality Interview

Getting It Right on Both Sides of the Mic

Tony Seton

Revised Edition

August 2011

This book is based on personal experience, interviews, discussions with colleagues, and additional research. The original version of this book was written and produced in 2006 and included suggested interview areas, primarily for politicians in that election. While many of those issues remain current, this version is published without those questions to make it more accessible to more people wanting to conduct a quality interview, inside and outside of politics.

The Quality Interview

2011 Revised Edition
Original Copyright 2006

All Rights Reserved

Published by TonySeton.com
ISBN-10: 146373493X
ISBN-13: 978-1463734930

Printed in the United States of America

Table of Contents

Notes

Of course there are both men and women involved in interviewing, on *Both Sides of the Mic*. The first draft of *The Quality Interview* included a haphazard mixed use of genders. That was just too confusing. So I went back through the text and vanilla-ized all of the pronouns that weren't specific to a person. There are male pronouns, royal we's and the generic they's. This is done for simplicity sake and no one should dare be offended. "You" are in this book, sometimes as a reader, and sometimes as an interviewer or interviewee.

A special thank you to Denise Swenson for her proofreading and polishing of this book.

Introduction

The information in this guide derives from more than forty-five years of journalism, including watching, producing, editing, and conducting interviews. So that you know from whence this information flows, I humbly include a sketchy view of my background.

A veteran broadcast journalist, I began my formal career on April Fools Day 1970 as a desk assistant on the overnight shift of the ABC Network Television News Assignment Desk in New York. During that decade, I worked my way up through the ranks, leaving ABC twice for interim opportunities. In various production capacities, primarily for ABC, I covered five space shots, six elections, Watergate, Barbara Walters' news interviews, and breaking news stories across North America. I won a handful of national awards for producing business/economics coverage for ABC. Later I wrote, produced, directed, and reported two award-winning public television programs: *Mother Nurture* and *Divorce – Collaborative Style.*

My radio credentials, beyond my parallel work at ABC television, include hosting a weekly call-in program on

KNRY (Monterey), directing sales and research at KXDC (Monterey), briefly hosting *InFormation with Tony Seton* (San Francisco) and earning the highest market ratings for my *Newsmaker* interviews and *SetonnoteS* commentaries on KQMS (Redding). I also filled in as host on a number of occasions on All-American Talk Radio, a nationally-syndicated program.

As a writer, I have published more than a dozen other books, including an industry handbook called *Don't Mess with the Press / How to Write, Produce and Report Quality Television News* (New York 2003). Some of the material in this book came from that book. In addition I have written more than 2,000 *SetonnoteS* commentaries, plus myriad other pieces ranging from political essays to poetry, some of which have found their way into publications across the country.

In addition to the broadcasting, I have extensive experience in marketing, advertising, public relations – from design to dissemination. And I've spent a considerable time in politics. In 1995, I co-founded *Wins of Change*, a political consulting firm whose clients included then-Congresswoman and later House Speaker Nancy Pelosi (D-San Francisco) and the American Nurses Association. I also consulted with Congressman Tom Campbell (R-Silicon Valley), in his two campaigns for United States Senate and a run for the California governorship. Plus there was a bunch of local candidates and issue campaigns on which I worked.

I launched the Quality News Network and on January 2nd 2006 we began delivering the finest hourly newscasts in the country. We also started a series of Special

Guest interviews, featuring conversations with a 2008 Presidential candidate, a frisbee-throwing psychiatrist, California''s Finance Chief, the brightest woman in the world, and various other interesting people.

In March 2006, I began a series of Candidates Interviews, which by the end of August had involved more than 250 candidates – mostly Congressional challengers – from all 50 states.

For fourteen months, I was the producer and correspondent for *America Back on Track* – a daily hour of news, interviews, and commentary – that aired locally and via satellite to stations across the country.

After QNN closed in 2008 for lack of business sense, I involved myself in consulting and writing. As of this writing, I have just published four novels in four months and should have a fifth out soon.

When I'm not writing or recording, I shoot photographs (mostly) of nature, walk by the Pacific Ocean, and occasionally ply the California skies as an (instrument-rated) private pilot.

Tony Seton
Monterey, California
August 2011

Why a Book on Interviewing

Interviews are ubiquitous in today's society. From the Sunday morning political talk circuit to people trying to get jobs, interviews are the currency of our information society. Of course, we don't think of most exchanges as interviews *per se*. Mostly, the word interview is in the context of news, but that range might extend from the frenetic happenstanceful witness to an accident, to often-pedantic morning briefings at the White House.

Interviews are vital to discovery and creativity. They foster a sharing of ideas and greater understanding. Well, they're supposed to, most of the time; sometimes they're designed to obfuscate and deceive. But even in those circumstances, if one side of the interview is committed to truth (justice and the American Way), a lot of valuable information and insight can be conveyed to the audience.

There are always three parties to an interview – the interviewer, the interviewee, and the audience. The first is theoretically a professional of some sort while the second might not be, though today even if they are not professionals, they are usually coached in how to answer anticipated questions. And the audience can be reading, listening and/or watching.

The purpose of this guide to *The Quality Interview* is to present some of the information garnered from more than four decades of experience about how to produce the most effective interview, *On Both Sides of the Mic*. In these pages you will find basic principles of interviewing, a discussion of techniques, and a potful of specific tips on how to accomplish the most efficient delivery of information.

This book will be valuable to interviewers – whether media professionals or HR executives – and to interviewees of every occupational and political stripe – especially authors, entertainers, and politicians on press tours. Knowing how an interview works from the other participant's perspective – how to organize information and present it effectively – can lead to a more productive collaboration.

According to a teacher who previewed this book, communications students are likely to find more of importance to their career than they will in most classrooms and regular textbooks. *The Quality Interview* will also be of interest to some of the general public, especially those who would like to understand how the interview dance is choreographed

Not all of the information within is of import to everyone – some of it is dryly technical – but it is a virtual certainty that a wide range of readers from journalism school students to public relations firms will learn something new.

A Guide to The Quality Interview

There are some basic ground rules to making a good interview, for people *on Both Sides of the Mic*. They are roughly broken down into what the interviewer and the interviewee need to know. In truth, both would benefit from knowing about the other's perspective. After the basics, the book gets into some of the finer points that arise in some interview situations but which won't be significant to all practitioners. For instance, you may never do an interview outside and need to worry about the angle of the sun or a windscreen. On the other hand, you might be a candidate who has just won a major upset and Scott Pelley wants to interview you from Washington. A sound engineer sticks an earpiece in your appropriate orifice and tells you it's an SAR. Will you know how to handle that?

There are many different types of interviews ranging from finding employment to prying information out of a witness. But most of the interviews discussed in *The Quality Interview* are the sort conducted by journalists for the news media. These are print or broadcast for the most part, with the latter encompassing radio, television and the Internet. There are differences among the media, of course. You don't have to worry about pictures with radio the way you do with television. The Internet is a hybrid that can include audio and/or video, though a lot of it is just print. For the pencil press, i.e., newspapers and magazines, you usually have a chance to "correct" what you say, which is often not an option in broadcasting, even when it's taped.

There are obvious differences between interviews that are recorded for broadcast or note-taking; those that are live versus recorded for playback; and those that are played in full or are conducted merely to collect just a sound bite or a quote. Rather than breakdown every point to every type of interview, in most cases it will be left to the reader to determine applicability to their own circumstances.

Even if you are not especially concerned with one particular section of this book or another, it is a short volume and if you read through it you are guaranteed to be exposed to a number of useful tips, both do's and don't's, which may one day turn the risk of a sorrowful performance into a grandiose exposition on important issues.

Not every situation is covered, of course. If you have questions that aren't answered, you are welcome to contact the author and we may incorporate the issues in the next version of this book. There will always be more to add.

If you do read all the way through, you will find some points are repeated, mostly because they are made in different contexts. Some are points that need to be underscored. It's like asking the same question two or more times during an interview, phrasing it slightly differently, in an attempt to evoke a different answer, or the same answer expressed in a different way. 'Tis the nature of the interview beast.

Also, being that this guide includes lots of bits of advice that don't require context so much as common sense, you will find in some places more a series of points rather than a narrative. That's what happens when there are many pieces of advice to deliver and it can be done in just a sentence or two.

Ultimately, this book is premised on the need for quality interviews with political candidates that will provide the American people with a better understanding of the issues and a better sense of which candidates are most likely to best address those issues. Most candidates these days are only given a cursory look by the media, unless there is scandal in the air. It seems that most media are more interested in selling time and space for political ads than in truly vetting those who seek public office. Symbiotically, candidates don't expect to be asked a lot of probing questions on the critical issues of the day.

Introduction

The main reason people are sought for media interviews is for the interviewer to elicit information from the interviewee. It is to get them to say on air or between quotation marks what might otherwise be part of a reporter's script. The interview brings special significance to the reporting because the content comes directly from a player in the story. In a sense, the purpose of an interview is not to elicit new information, but to make a better news report. Which is a good thing if it attracts more of an audience and increases their awareness of the issues.

There are several primary reasons why an interviewee consents to an interview. One is to get out information favorable to his cause, image, product, etc., as in, "My new book...." Another purpose is to mitigate information unfavorable to his cause, as in, "He really stopped beating Missus Caesar fairly early on."

Other people do interviews because they like the limelight, or because by granting access to themselves, they can better control their exposure. This is true of celebrities as well as of business or political types.

If there is another reason it might be that the interviewer wants to rub shoulders with the interviewee, figuratively speaking. Many interviewers are all about "the get", that is, that they are speaking with someone making headlines, rather than in getting into any depth about why they are making news.

Interviews come in all shapes and sizes. There's the quickie on-the-street-job: asking an eyewitness what he saw. There's the extended version with a politician or civic leader. There's the neo-scripted Sunday morning Washington gabfest which often seems less like an actual evocation of information and more like a cross between a wailing Greek chorus and kabuki mime. Lots of talking, cheerleading, moaning but rarely anything new said.

Then there is the considerably more rare form of inter-view – what one politician-turned-journalist pal called "a real interview" in which useful, important, honest information is transferred to readers or listeners in an engaging – sometimes even enthralling – conversation. Bill Moyers did it with Joseph Campbell in *The Power of Myth* and James Lipton does it often *Inside the Actor's Studio*. A good interview is one that reaches the high standard suggested by Marshall McLuhan when he spoke of the inextricable entwining of education and entertainment.

As a listener, you know a good interview because it not only informs but it stimulates your own thinking, taking you further in your awareness of an idea or a person; or by elucidating a subject and giving you a better understanding of it, gives you a better under-standing of yourself.

A good interview is usually a two-person affair; that's where you can get down to it, so to speak. The best interviews are conducted by people who are genuinely interested in finding out information that is of interest to their audience. Those are interviews with people who are at least willing – and sometimes anxious – to share that interesting information, preferably for purposes other than to manipulate audience opinion. When both vessels are free of sediment, the flow can be sparklingly clear.

Interviews are conducted in order to convey a message to a larger audience. They can be with an author to promote his book sales, with an elected official to allay his constituents' fears, or with a CEO responding to accusations that one of his company's products is carcinogenic. From the interviewee's point of view, the purpose of an interview is to use the media to reach and sway either a mass or target audience.

A press release, billboard, newspaper ad or broadcast campaign may catch more eyes and ears, but an interview usually carries more credibility. The interviewer is representing the public's need (or interest) to know, and as such, will ask questions that evoke the responses the audience wants to hear. After all, that's why people tuned in, and all too often the audience is disappointed when the interviewer fails to ask the right questions, or when the interviewee is allowed to get away with lies, evasion, spin, or softball answers.

Keep that in mind the next time you listen to a full-fledged interview, or even when you catch just a sound cut on the news. Did you find out what you wanted to know? Were the answers typical public-relations responses? Was the person just staying on message? Was it a sales pitch? Was it believable? Did you want to hear more? Did the interviewer do his job well?

Depending on the quality of the questioner, the viewers and listeners may or may not hear what's actually important. Too often, the audience must sit through the detritus of talking points, only to find themselves still hungering for the facts; the kind that will help them truly understand current events.

The quality of an interview is defined by both what is and what is not asked and answered. If both participants are committed to the process, the audience can glean a great deal of information and insight. But varying levels of competence, honesty, and private agendas often get in the way of a quality interview.

Take, for instance, an author doing an interview to promote his latest book. Most book-tour interviews are benign, pre-packaged affairs. The author is shuttled hither and yon, talking to as many people as his publicist can line up. The same questions tend to be asked over and over again, (necessarily) causing the author to lose interest. As a result, the answers come out canned and they lose their intended punch. With the often over-worked, underpaid and severely-disinterested interviewer reading questions from press kits, what could have been interesting turns into perfunctory slush.

The same goes for politicians and civic leaders who are trying to convince the public to support an idea that doesn't succeed on the obvious merits. It's an uphill battle, with most combatants depending on carefully crafted thirty-second TV messages to move public opinion, rather than providing honest talk and straight-forward logic. That's because the politicians can control the content of the purchased time, the way it's presented, and the accompanying visuals.

But in an interview, politicians and civic leaders are, to some degree, at the mercy of the interviewer, who may or may not be sympathetic, may or may not have all the pertinent facts, and may or may not be knowledgeable.

The current landscape of news programs, talk shows and print interviews is heavily dependent on interviews to ostensibly inform their audiences. The more you understand how those interviews are conducted the better you will be able to effectively assimilate what is being presented, deliberately and otherwise.

For the Interviewer

Interviewing is an art. Whether you make your living at it as Bill Moyers did producing hour upon hour for PBS, or you're a reporter who needs a sound bite to flesh out a minute-thirty local news spot on the ribbon cutting at a new sewage plant, the purpose is to elicit comments that will help to tell a story. The better interviewer knows his role is to evoke the response rather than distract the audience with the question.

That flies in the face of the practices of some of our most famous interviewers, some of whom tend to overshadow their guests. Larry King, Barbara Walters, Ted Koppel, and others draw famous names and sizeable audiences. That doesn't mean that they always ask the most important questions or produce the most significant answers.

When Barbara Walters traveled to Berlin for an interview with German Chancellor Helmut Schmidt, I was her producer. Barbara told Schmidt that he should keep his answers short. Schmidt responded, "You American reporters always ask long questions and want short answers." He might have been thinking of

Ted Koppel, the excruciatingly well-informed former host of ABC's *Nightline* for several decades who was notorious for asking very lengthy questions, especially, it seemed, when coming out of the last commercial. He would preface his questions with, "We only have a few seconds left..."

What's true about the good reporter, famous or not, is that he is listening first. Instead of formulating the next question, he is thinking ahead in terms of how what he is hearing might be used, or not, in his report. The best reporters hear the in-cues and the out-cues of the sound cuts they will insert in their story while the interviewees are speaking. Some even hear in their mind's ear what they will write to lead into or out of those sound bites. They do this while still listening; multitasking, before the word was even imagined.

Good print reporters listen in a similar fashion, although they usually have more space for more quotes and they don't have to worry about the quality of the sound recording or what kind of pictures they might use to illuminate the story, beyond words.

For all reporters, the heavy lifting is done while the tape is rolling. By the time they get to editing their story, their options are limited. If it was a good interview, grand. If it wasn't, well, some cutting, some pasting, some words of explanation...So reporters must take advantage of the opportunities that present themselves during the interview to shape the final piece.

For broadcasters, there is an obvious difference between live and tape; you can sometimes fix the latter.

But often not. Especially full programs that are produced in pattern; that is, they are recorded as if they were live, the same way they will be aired. So there is little opportunity to pull things out or add later.

Much of news reporting today consists of quickie interviews – ten minutes or less. The tape is hand-carried or fed back to the studio, and a small chunk of sound winds up being inserted into the full report. Knowing that can take the edge off of the questioning. Take two, take three...I didn't get what I wanted so I'll ask the question again. When you have plenty of time and tape, you can get lazy. The more you get used to presuming that you are always live, the less room there is for mistakes.

If you are doing an interview by rote, asking questions to which you presume to already have the answers, you undercut your interviewee and limit what you might get out of the interview. Letting your mind wander to your script or article or an upcoming weekend doesn't preclude your getting an appropriate answer, but it makes getting the optimum sound cut or quote unlikely. Just think what it is like talking to your co-workers or friends when they're distracted.

This note of codification. It's one thing to quickly realize that a sound cut works perfectly in your script. It's another to allow yourself to be distracted from the interview.

In some ways interviewing is less a matter of showing up with a sheet full of questions and more an exercise in being present. That's what real listening is about. You need to be able to read the other person, to put him at ease, to elicit the information in a way that viewers will understand.

It is important with all interviewees – from professional speakers such as politicians to first-timers such as man-on-the-street's – to develop a rapport with them before anything else. With first-time interviewees, let them know you are not dangerous by engaging in conversation and making them feel comfortable with you as a person. If you don't have a better opportunity such as a pre-interview meeting, take the time when you are sitting down with them and the cameraman or photographer is getting his lighting and focus right.

So a key point to interviewing is to relax, on both sides of the microphone. Even in a situation where eliciting the target information could be contentious, remember that this is more a game than a battle, and more like tennis than rugby. Show your interviewee your peace of mind. It really is contagious. Some interviewers say nothing to their "victims" until just before the camera begins rolling or their pen goes to paper. That approach is often counterproductive. Instead, talk to the person, let him hear your voice, cadence, tone. If you are calm, not surreptitiously looking for a secret, unhurried but vibrant, you will raise the communication level, making the interview and whatever comes out of it more productive.

Most people who are being interviewed are concerned about two things: how they look, and how they sound – their actual voice and/or their words and thoughts. The first part can usually be taken care of by telling them to sit comfortably, and by making an attentive and approving scan of the scene. If you're doing a television interview, set it up so that the interviewee sits with his feet on the ground and his eyes are level with the camera lens. Making this point to the interviewee shows him that you have his interests at heart.

You might also note to him that butterflies in the stomach before you go on-air is normal, and even appropriate; the audience is tuning in to listen to him deliver information of import and interest. In truth, many talented broadcast professionals have to deal with their own knotted nerves every time they put themselves before a camera or behind a microphone, but the butterflies usually disappear moments after they begin speaking.

The perfect delivery resonates with confidence tempered by humility. You want to be knowledgeable, and sound like you are, but not to the point of coming off as superior. As you look into the camera and begin to speak, you want to appear professional and maybe even a little honored to be allowed into your viewer's living room.

The most effective interviewers truly engage their guests, preferably on the given subjects. Even for those interviewees who don't really want to be there, their contributions will be more authentic if they are made comfortable. When questioning someone, either for just a sound bite or for an extended interview, you will get more out of him when you empower him and impart the importance of his role in the report.

One of the ways to put people at ease in a broadcast interview is to make the camera and microphones less intrusive – that way, the guest can focus more easily on the conversation. For example, two lavalier micro-phones, the kind that clip on to the clothes, are much less distracting than you reaching back and forth with a hand-held microphone.

You might also tell your guest that you have plenty of tape and that he should stop and restart an answer if he doesn't feel he has made himself clear. Again, the purpose of the interview is to get the interviewee to say something significant in a concise and illuminating manner.

The more you can make the interview a dialogue, the more the interviewee will be willing to contribute. Too often, reporters will act self-importantly and offend the interviewee, reducing his willingness to cooperate. Whether it is overt or subtle, cooperation makes all the difference. The interviewer doesn't have to make friends with the guest, but the more comfortable the relationship on both sides, the better will be the interview product.

*   *   *   *   *   *

An example of how an interview can go wrong when the sides are not in accord is drawn from the Senate Watergate Hearings. Joseph Montoya, a Democrat from New Mexico, put Nixon counselor John Ehrlichman in a very bad light and it wasn't Ehrlichman's fault. Ehrlichman – a deliberately contentious fellow despite the circumstances of the hearings – was in control throughout most of his testimony. But when it came time to field questions from Montoya, Ehrlichman hit a snag. Montoya confused his facts, and when the witness, Ehrlichman, charged that Montoya was mixing apples and oranges, Montoya erupted and filleted Ehrlichman before a national television audience. As Ehrlichman's attorney later said, a bad questioner can make even a good answerer look bad.

A more common problem arises when the person being interviewed makes an ineffective presentation. For example, the majority of engineers, doctors, researchers, and scientists are all well known for their inability to speak in generic terms. Also, many normally articulate people freeze up during an interview and forget everything they were going to say. They may have nothing to hide, but their verbal clumsiness – combined with deer-in-the-headlights look on their faces – create a poor impression.

When you are interviewing people who are unfamiliar with the process, offer some suggestions. For example, tell them to answer in complete sentences, or to incorporate your questions into their answers. If you ask, "Do you think the colt will ever be able to race, and when?" and the answer comes back , "Yeah. Six months," you can be in something of jam in the edit room. But if the answer is, "I think the colt will be able to race in six months," you'll have a lot more latitude when it's time to cut your piece. Very few people remember to do this after the second or third question, but providing them with this framework can help some people to think not only about the question but also about their answer.

Indeed, with some people it is useful to suggest that they think about what they are going to say before responding. Virtually all stories have a beginning, middle, and end. Tell them to start at the beginning.

That said, some people think better on their feet, without time to consider what they have to say. Whatever works; that is why it is worth the time to get to know the basics of how the interviewee thinks and reacts before the interview starts.

*　　*　　*　　*　　*　　*

Humor is a good way to ease the tension. You might joke that the first thing you'll ask them is to confirm that they are not doing the interview under duress. (Unless they are, of course.) People will often open up about feeling uncomfortable, and you can then address their specific concerns. Remove those concerns – e.g., lights in their eyes, whether they can start an answer over again – and a person's energy will quickly and dramatically change. The transformation is actually perceptible on tape.

There is scientific reasoning behind this emphasis on forming a relationship with the interviewee. In his book, "The Silent Pulse," George Leonard describes a scientific experiment that examined how people listen. Using high-speed photography, researchers filmed two people, one speaking and one listening. Then they parsed the film into the smallest units of sound. For instance, the word "ask" had five separate sounds in it. And what they discovered was that during each of the five separate sounds, the speaker exhibited a different set of body movements.

More significantly, the listener also exhibited five separate sets of body movements in perfect synch with the speaker. This underscores how important it is to listen to the people you are interviewing. The more you entrain them in the conversation, the more likely you are to get the thoughtful answers you seek.

* * * * * *

The substance of an interview is almost always what is said, as opposed to visuals or sound factors. And, while you have questions and expect answers, neither you nor your guest is working from a fixed script; most of the time. Unlike feature interviews with major public figures who are used to being interviewed, most news interviews are less structured. For one thing, you have less control over what the novice interviewee will say, or how; they don't know the rules, so to say.

If the interviewee says something outrageous, you have several options, depending on what is said. If there is the possibility of following this up, you might continue the conversation with, "You seem serious. How do you back up such a statement?" Another option is to just say, "Thank you" and wait for more. Or you can simply ignore the remark. If it is totally inappropriate you might say, "This doesn't serve our viewers," and take the microphone away. (If you're doing television, direct the cameraman to also turn the camera away.

Sometimes you have to offer a little more leeway with an interviewee who seems to have pushed the credibility envelope too far. Especially with a public figure, and particularly with a politician who has painted himself into a corner and is dancing around admitting a mistake. Other times the person will be so wrapped up in his deceit that he refuses to tell the truth. During the crumbling of his denial of his affair with Monica Lewinsky, Bill Clinton suggested at a news conference that the word "is" as in "is having a relationship," was open for interpretation. Normally such denial or obfuscation needs to be pursued in such a case, but in a situation like that silence is golden. The perp has hung himself, and no one is going to cut him down.

*   *   *   *   *   *

Know your topic. Ask your questions directly, and freshly. Though you may presume to know what to expect, any such intimation undercuts the very reason for the interview. When you express genuine interest in the story, the interviewee will usually respond in kind. Or, in a combative situation, he may be thrown off balance by your directness and reveal himself. You may not get the bank president to say, "Yes I did it," when you ask if he knows who embezzled the $250,000, but his face or body language may say more than words.

Should your interviewee know in advance what are going to be your questions? Rarely will anyone show up for an interview without having at least a general sense of what is going to be asked. A good interviewer will have questions either written down or in his head, but he will use those questions as a stepping off point and will ask follow-ups based on the answers he receives.

Some reporters adamantly refuse to reveal the questions they intend to ask before the interview. This might make sense in the rare case where the interviewee doesn't know what the interviewer knows and is going to ask, but those people are rarely likely to consent to the interview in the first place. When setting up the interview, outline to the interviewee the subjects you want to discuss. In most cases, the interviewee will know the gist of the questions anyway, so laying out the questions beforehand will help to allay any fear of surprises.

You also don't have to provide all of the questions you intend to ask in advance. If the interviewee decides he doesn't want to answer that question, he can say so outright or come off as evasive. It's not likely he will say, "Hey, that wasn't what you said you were going to ask," though such comments have certainly been captured on tape. Ultimately, an interviewee might storm out, but that would be rare and excessive. And it could make for its own story.

*   *   *   *   *   *

Be patient. Don't be in a rush to jump in on the answer. Particularly in poignant interviews on television, the face should be given a chance to finish expressing what the words have said. When a person switches from talking to listening, the internal focus of his attention shifts and the expression changes, sometimes prematurely. So wait a beat for the interviewee to fully digest his own answer to one question, before asking another. Watch the person's eyes; most times they will shift when the response is complete. You can also see this when you are back in the editing room, if the shot is tight enough. It can make for dramatic visuals.

You will often go into interviews already knowing the answers to some of the questions. But when you have the time, and if you ask the right questions, you can sometimes draw some unexpected remarks out of people which they themselves did not expect to say.

Everyone has a story after all. Sometimes the meatiest part of an interview will appear when the person being interviewed is asked a question that he didn't expect, or the reporter steers the conversation into unfamiliar territory.

You owe it to your audience to get even a guarded interviewee to speak honestly and clearly. This is not always easy if the person has something to hide, and especially with well-trained public figures. But you can sometimes get people to let down their guard by being honest about the information that you seek, and by looking them in the eyes when they answer, rather than down at your notes.

However, some people do get nervous with eye contact so you may have to look at your notes to give them space to think and speak. But for the most part, you will want to look at the person until he has finished speaking. It is respectful, and it makes sense visually to the audience. After he has answered your question, look down at your notes if you need to, though follow-up questions will often flow from the answers, and most times you will already have in mind other questions that need to be asked.

* * * * * *

Whenever possible and appropriate, ask questions that probe beneath the surface. For instance, I was producing a Dan Cordtz interview with a Bank of America executive whose answers sounded like they had been frequently delivered. It wasn't that he was being evasive; he just seemed overly familiar with the information. So I asked him what was new about the circumstances he was seeing today, as opposed to twenty years ago. Suddenly he came alive; there was a new energy in his voice. He had been invited to think for himself instead of repeating familiar thoughts, and he did so openly and visually.

You can get people to say the most fascinating things when you sincerely ask for their opinions. Expressing a real interest in their own professional (or personal) assessment of a situation can open them right up. Some of the best sound cuts have come in response to questions like:

"What do you see that is different now from when this happened previously?"

"What is it going to mean?"

"Why should people care about what's happening?"

"What do you see as the most significant element of this situation?"

"Where does that put us now?"

*   *   *   *   *   *

It isn't appropriate to deliberately make someone look stupid or uninformed. An exception might be when someone is in a position to do serious damage. In that case, exposing him as unknowledgeable or incapable could be a public service.

Asking questions involving minutiae are usually seen as trying to show up the interviewee. This happened to candidate George Bush in 2000 when he was asked who were the leaders of some very small, marginally-significant countries and he didn't know. There are presumptions made in all cases about a person's knowledge, and nibbling around the edges is unprofessional, unless the person being interviewed is pretending to know more than he actually does. Even then, however, it is not the role of the interviewer, as a matter of course, to try to show up an interviewee.

When you open things up with a more in-depth question, make sure to stay within the interviewee's scope of knowledge. This may sound obvious, but a reporter will often ask someone to comment on something, not knowing that it is beyond that person's purview or knowledge. "Do you think the company is being run well?" is a fine question for a presidential candidate, but not a wise thing to ask a guard at the visitor's center. The guard will probably have his own opinions and may even be willing to voice them, but in most cases, his opinion will not be usefully informed.

*   *   *   *   *   *

With the expansion of news operations and coverage, many more people in public life and on the fringes of celebrity have had experience with television news people. Many companies provide media training and conduct seminars for their press people and executives so that they know how to handle hostile questions from Mike Wallace, Geraldo Rivera, or their emulators. Such training is of questionable valuable since so often the purpose is not to tell the truth but to hide it, and that is almost always apparent. Also, it's usually the simple question and the simple answer that, taken out of context or mis-edited, puts yolk on the corporate seal.

Be wary of people who earn their keep by talking to the

press – especially those who try to take control of the interviews. One familiar ploy is to pretend that you and he are friends:

"Well, Frank, I'm glad you asked me that question, because you know me, and you know those charges couldn't possibly be true."

The purpose of using your first name and asserting a relationship is to give the interviewee credibility with your listeners. It also undercuts your impartiality in the minds of the viewers. If you are going into an interview with someone you know enough to be on a first-name basis, tell them you want to maintain formality and to not give the impression that you are friends. After all, he's not there as your friend. (One exception to this rule is with children.)

Many times you will see in someone who is being interviewed that he is thinking about the most effective – for his purposes – answer to your question. If you allow him to get away with a series of couched statements that avoid the important points, you've merely handed him the microphone. But if you can get underneath the veneer, and ask your questions with the weight of his constituents behind you, you can sometimes force a less-varnished version of the truth.

Don't badger an interviewee if he won't answer your question. Try rephrasing the question. If the guest still seems reluctant to respond, simply ask why. If he doesn't have the information, let him off the hook. If it's information he should have but doesn't, ask where it can be found. Interviews are exchanges of ideas, not battles. No one should win.

Brow-beating is unprofessional and impolite. As a reporter, you represent the public and its right to know. Being a professional means you will conduct a dignified interview. It can be frustrating when your interviewee is holding back or being deceitful, but that never gives you permission to ask unfair questions.

If someone isn't telling the truth, it usually comes across in their facial expressions, tone of voice, and/or body language. If they are being evasive or simply refuse to answer, you can sometimes explain what information you want and ask how the question might be re-framed in order to elicit an answer. If the person is a crook, he still won't comply, but sometimes the interviewee is merely confused by the question.

When you come up against someone who is being evasive, remain professionally courteous, but press your point. Ask him how he thinks the situation might be interpreted by the average viewer, and what might he say to help them understand. Point out mitigating factors and ask if the tables were turned, might he find his own answer – ahem – difficult to swallow. You never want to call someone a liar, but if the person is not telling the truth, your questions and his answers should reveal the fact.

Don't be rude, but don't let your interviewee be rude to you, either. The fact that you have sought the interview implies that he has something to say. His agreement to do the interview says that he is willing for you to record what he has to say, and that puts the ball in your court. You have the right to ask your questions so long as you are professional about it.

*   *   *   *   *   *

Try not to interrupt a guest during an interview. There are exceptions. You can do so politely if he doesn't seem to understand your question, or he gets off on an irrelevancy or tries to filibuster. He should be told in advance that the shorter he keeps his answers the more ground you will be able to cover. And in most interview situations, he will know what you are going to discuss. If you're taping and the person begins rambling, you might ask the cameraman or director to stop the tape and then re-instruct the interviewee on how best to conduct the interview.

If you are live, you have to be more judicious. For instance, you might wait until the camera is on the guest, and show the director a subtle "cut" sign. By prior arrangement, that should mean cutting the guest's mic and coming to you. If the guest doesn't behave in a reasonable manner, go to a commercial and don't come back to the studio until you have regained control. This isn't about ego, it's about professional conduct and access to the airwaves.

*   *   *   *   *   *

Don't be awed by titles. Whether you are interviewing the President of the United States or a Hollywood actor, if the person has consented to an interview, he has put himself in your hands as the interviewer. You both have your roles to play. Your position with the mayor should be the same as with a kindergartner: respectful and confident, attentive and discerning.

When interviewing a professional answerer, i.e. a public relations or press relations specialist, you can sometimes find yourself in a difficult position of trying to get significant information out of him when he's not willing to provide it. It can be immensely frustrating when dealing with a professional who can say nothing very well, or make his client look the victim of an inquisition. Sometimes you can outline the information you don't get from the spokesman in the introduction or the text following the interview.

Make sure that you aren't used by a company or an organization. Don't let them put their spin on a story when you know it will obfuscate the issues or deceive your audience. You are better to keep them off your air entirely than to let them control the flow or accuracy of information to your readers, listeners or viewers.

*   *   *   *   *   *

Always assume your audience is smarter than the general public. Think of how you have explained a familiar television program to someone who has come in after the program has started. He understands the essential framework; you are catching him up on the details. With that posture in mind, you come off as guiding rather than condescending. That's usually the best approach to take with your audience.

Condescension has a greater impact on a visceral level than cognitive. Looking down on your viewers is not something you can hide, so if you ever find yourself doing it, you can assume you've already offended a number of them. They may change the channel or tune in to another station without you even knowing why.

If you ever find yourself feeling superior, take some time off. It's important to remember that you probably have more information than does your audience, which is the reason they are watching. They may not be as smart as you, but they're the ones with the remote controls. Also, it's your job to inform, not just report. Remember that these are the public airwaves, so practice humility and deliver the goods.

It is also wise to make every effort to keep emotion out of your voice. While some stories may pull at your heartstrings, don't share that with your viewers. Likewise, when you're covering a boring subject, enliven your attitude while writing the script – and certainly before you deliver it. Remember that much of the communication between yourself and your viewers is non-verbal, and they will be able to pick up on the fact that a story bores you if you let the fact come through.

A Harvard study conducted in the mid-80s found that 55% of a viewer's impression of an anchor came from his body language and facial expressions. Another 37% was generated by the tone of voice and other elements in the shot. Only 8% of the communication was conveyed through the actual words.

While those percentages may have changed somewhat over time, the concept still holds true. The results show that as good as your script may be, it is delivery, body language and intonation that can be the key to how your script is received. This is true whether you are anchoring a newscast or hosting an interview. The more you are able to neutralize the body language and intonation, the more power will be in your words.

When searching for the right manner in which to speak with your audience, assume you are dealing with a particular mindset – specifically, the ethos endemic to the community. People have specific beliefs about themselves and their neighbors, and the community may be so insular that shared attitudes are often not questioned or examined. Take the example of red states and blue states. People in the former are less likely to embrace homosexual marriages, a reproductive choice, a moratorium on oil drilling than are people in the latter. Awareness of who is watching can help tailor how you contextualize subjects and introduce guests.

Also, remember that the public does not necessarily have the same adoring (or even tolerant) view of television reporters as they did in the past. As a whole, journalism has gone downhill as many local stations dumbed down their content to reach a broader audience. The networks, too, have become less informing in their attempts to draw more viewers, opting for features as opposed to hard news. Consequently, since Walter Cronkite left the anchor at CBS in 1981, there has been a fifty percent decline in network news viewership. When you talk down to your audience, when you cease to deliver relevant coverage, the audience will go elsewhere.

To reverse this trend, interviewers, anchors, and reporters must present themselves to the public as objective, well-informed and self-aware – cognitively and viscerally, smoothly and professionally. If you find yourself working in a place where these qualities aren't respected – where you're asked to be a "personality" – and if you're serious about journalism, you'll probably be happier elsewhere.

*   *   *   *   *   *

If you are having trouble getting someone to speak freely, try changing your posture and asking the question in a more personal tone. Something like, "When you get home tonight, how will you characterize this interview to your wife?" You probably will not use the question or the ensuing answer, but just by thinking about that question, your interviewee will likely realize the importance of that moment in the interview. Or at least he will consider that the answer he gave might not be sufficient or adequately clear.

People who are unfamiliar with the interview process will frequently produce convoluted answers. If you get answers that are rambling or disjointed, ask the interviewee to restate his answers. With the information recently spoken, and thus closer to the front of their minds, they will often be able to re-assemble their thoughts more concisely. But this should only be done when the person's inability to form a coherent answer is not part of the story. For example, if you are interviewing a criminal about a crime, you don't want him to polish up his alibi.

Often a person will know the information but doesn't have a particular facility for delivering it. This is frequently the case with scientists, and with people who are inexperienced with the task of explaining matters. You might restate the question, suggesting that the audience might not have understood the answer in the way that it was phrased. Usually the interviewee will accept that explanation, especially if he is aware that he hadn't been clear. But with some people you have to explain it in those terms, or they could become suspicious of your intentions, .e.g., that you are trying to trap them. On the other hand, the person just might think that you yourself are not very bright and just did not understand his answer.

Cardinal rule: if you don't understand an answer, ask for clarification. If you don't understand it, neither will many of your viewers. Ask the same question differently to evoke another perspective, or repeat the question later; the interviewee may have shifted his thoughts and be able to answer more coherently.

* * * * * *

Even if you know what questions you want to ask, it is always good to have at least some questions or ideas jotted down. It is also smart to write down the interviewee's name at the top of the page. On a long shoot, you can draw a blank on a number, a fact, or even a person's name. It happens to the best of reporters.

* * * * * *

Protect your interviewee; don't ask stupid questions. Asking a mother who just lost her son in an accident, "Will you miss your son?" invites a predictable and useless answer. If you are trying to get the mother to describe her son – so viewers can more easily understand the depth of her loss – ask instead, "How was your son different from other children his age?" or "What will you miss most about him?" But such questions should have a purpose beyond trying to evoke emotions.

* * * * * *

If you do find yourself with a predictable answer on tape, and it doesn't add to the story, don't use it. For example, a neighbor could be commenting about the next-door mass murderer and say something like, "He was always such a nice boy," "Never heard a peep out of him," or "I always thought there was something odd about him." Those quotes contribute nothing to the story, except to imply that there was little or no communication going on in that neighborhood.

*   *   *   *   *   *

Interviewees are either those who have information they want to share, or others. The "others" include people who are willing to speak but are too nervous, sometimes to the point of silence. Also included are people who have information that they want to protect. This can be for a variety of reasons, some of them valid: humility, dignity, or common decency.

Others want to manipulate the interview to serve their own purposes. Some people in public relations, arrogant politicians, and celebrities seem to think and act as though they are doing you a favor by them granting an interview. The more adept interviewer will reveal this attitude to the audience in his questioning.

*   *   *   *   *   *

These are some other things to keep in mind during the interview:

-- Identify your guest several times, by name and reason for being there, especially after any breaks for commercials or news, .e.g., "We're speaking with...."

-- Give your guest the opportunity to provide

contact information at least once, and if only once, at the end of the interview.

-- Avoid rapid-fire questions; give the guest a chance to answer. Sometimes you can ask a series of questions that the guest can then answer in a long, cohesive piece. For instance, "Tell us about that night, were you tired, what were the road conditions, what was the weather."

-- Give your own opinions sparingly. Remember who the expert is and that he is your guest.

-- Time your humor so as to not deflate a guest's statement.

-- Don't intentionally embarrass guests. Sometimes they will do this themselves. Don't let them "twist slowly, slowly in the wind."

For the Interviewee

As noted earlier, people consent to interviews for a variety of reasons: to explain a pressing situation, to share knowledge, to sell a book or a film or themselves. Their effectiveness is based on the forum, the facts, and the ability of the participants to get out the information. We know that many talk show hosts are simply entertainers who are filling time, while a small number are genuinely interested in sharing important information with their listeners. Similarly, the motivations of interviewees can range from nobility to greed.

The venues for their expression varies significantly. Some people go on the after-hours talk shows to expose themselves as depraved idiots, though they probably wouldn't express their intentions in quite those words. Indeed, watching Judge Judy-type programs, it's a wonder that the civilization has survived with some of those folks who are walking our Earth. A step up was Oprah, who while still playing for a visceral reaction, usually got some useful information out to her viewers.

There are myriad opportunities every day on radio and

television, the Internet and print, for people to tell their stories to credible interviewers. They can be merely informative, and sometimes stimulating. There are such programs on in cities across the country, on both public and commercial stations and other outlets. The focus of this book is these more substantial interviews.

*   *   *   *   *   *

Interviews are often the venue of choice for business people or politicians who are trying to get out from under a cloud. For example, Bill and Hillary Clinton went on *Sixty Minutes* during his 1992 presidential run to confront reports that he had been a bit too affectionate with Gennifer Flowers. The interview was largely a success because, while most viewers probably thought he was "guilty," Mr. Clinton charmed them into thinking it didn't matter.

This particular process involved considerable irony. Hillary Clinton accompanied her husband to make him more credible among women; her appearance at his side may have been intended to suggest some sort of new, feminist acceptance of philandering. It was also cattily suggested that because the public got a good look at her, some people would understand, sympathetically, why her husband had strayed.

The Enron trial in 2006 illuminated the problem of many interviewees. Executives Kenneth Lay and Jeffrey Skilling took the stand in their own defense, but according to comments made later by jurors, that was a mistake. Lay and Skilling presented themselves badly and that contributed to their convictions. The whole Enron story reeked of arrogance, both when the company was successful and when it failed. That attitude was witnessed by the jury and hurt the defendants. Had they realized how they were being seen, they might have changed their posture. As it was, Lay said he was shocked by the verdict.

Most interviews do not involve such high stakes, of course. Many interviews between a businessman and reporter are aimed at taking the sting out of lowered earnings reports, explaining the overnight failure of an over-hyped product, or announcing a willingness to cooperate with a newly-launched investigation by the Securities and Exchange Commission.

When there's no way to avoid bad news, it's best to have an honest, credible person get it out as quickly as possible. The expression KISS – Keep It Simple Stupid – is highly appropriate in these matters. The communication is clearer when the audience is presented with the facts, rather than having to dig through layer after layer of obfuscation, or even over-explanation. And the best person to deliver the facts is the person in charge, competently and unreluctantly answering questions posed by the interviewer.

For instance, consider how much fallout resulted from the delay and manner in which Vice President Dick Cheney's shooting incident came to light in 2006. If he had come forward himself at the time of the shooting, there would have been little issue of a possible cover-up. Instead, many people never believed Cheney's belated – and implausible – explanation of what had occurred.

Another example is Bill Clinton's admission during the

1992 presidential campaign that he had smoked marijuana in college, but didn't inhale. By doing this, he opened himself up to ridicule that never went away. Tens of millions of Americans have smoked pot, and it's not a big deal for most people. With his inept response, Clinton did himself more damage than if he'd just said, "Yes, I smoked pot."

When disaster strikes, the top official of the enterprise or organization suffering the hit should acknowledge the bad news immediately and – as the situation warrants – outline an aggressive and reasoned response to problems. The next step is to set new goals, as well as a practical timetable for both correcting the problems and implementing new protocol for avoiding a recurrence.

(There are occasions when someone other than the boss should do the explaining. For instance, if the top person is particularly inarticulate, or if he has to be on the scene of the event. In those circumstances, find a higher-up with good communications skills who will be trusted by the audience.)

When delivering bad news, don't be steely or defensive but you have to show some pain. Otherwise, you are implying that you are just a mouthpiece for the real crooks and have nothing personal at stake. The audience will be left feeling that the boss remains insulated from the real results.

There is an old saw that says, "Fool me once and you're the fool; but fool me twice and I'm the fool." The public doesn't want to be taken for a fool. They won't be receptive to you coming back for understanding and forgiveness a second time.

*   *   *   *   *   *

If you're doing the interview to generate a response, tell the audience what you want them to do. Be clear, and be simple. Don't come up with a laundry list of options. Stick to one or two actions. If you want them to call a congressman's office, say so, recite the number, and tell them where else they can find it. It is most practical to send people to a website.

If you want them to attend a rally on Main Street, tell them the day and time at least twice. Remember, most people listening to the radio – eighty percent by most estimates – are passive. If you want them to do something, set your expectations low. You shouldn't require much more effort than responding to an "applause" sign in a television studio. The active listeners are willing to put out some effort, but the less you ask them to do, the more likely they are to participate.

If you are doing the interview as a way to sell something, resist making an overt sales pitch. Obviously, if you are on a book tour, you want audience members to jump on Amazon and order a copy while you're still on the air, but you're more likely to sell those books if you just provide a taste of what they will find between the covers without actually suggesting that anyone actually purchase it.

Let the audience decide on its own whether to buy your product based on how exciting you make the kitchen-ware or how steamy the autobiography sounds. Don't insult their collective intelligence by suggesting that they will realize their dreams if only they plunk down money for your product. That's for infomercials.

The sales targets for interviews come in two distinct flavors: those who can use your product, and those who can't. The best strategy is to ensure that everyone who would be happy with the purchase understands it. If you do a good job, even people who don't actually need whatever it is you are selling will be enticed into buying it. But be careful, because after you have their money, they may decide later on down the line that they didn't like the book or never used the all-purpose cleaner – and they'll resent having been fooled, even if that was never your intention.

*   *   *   *   *   *

The listener call-in format can be a successful medium for many guests, depending on the parameters, the host, and the screener. Some of these programs aim to generate controversy, and encourage contentious callers whose sole purpose for calling is often just to rant.

If you put yourself into such a lion's den, here are some things to keep in mind. First, many callers are flattered when you use their names. But try not to be too obvious, or it can seem like pandering. You might say, "Thanks for your suggestion, Hannah," or, later in the conversation, mention to the host that Jane had a really good question about basmati rice...always a confrontational subject.

Another point about call-in shows, the people who call in are usually more interested in hearing themselves than actually having their questions answered. That means that the more questions you get to, the more people you make happy. Also, the audience appreciates it when you respond to more people, i.e., by taking more calls. So try to answer as many questions as time-efficiently as possible.

If you want to take a question and move the conversation in another direction, do so, but make sure the caller has gotten his due. Even if it's, "Laurel, that's a great question, but we don't really have the time to get into it in the depth it deserves. Let me say this...." You can then give the answer in a sentence or two, move on to another, more relevant issue, or take another call. Of course, if you are dealing with a confrontational host and hostile audience, you might go on at great length with your answer. Not to be punitive; perhaps they'll learn from you.

Speaking of confrontational, you will rarely win an argument with a contentious talk show host. He controls the audio. If he's invited you on his show to pick a fight, your best option is to decline. If you're ambushed, you could always play innocent with such lines as, "I thought you asked me here to talk." But folks who are rude on the air don't play by the rules. Since the host has his finger on your microphone button, he can play you like an instrument and make you look like a fool or incompetent.

An adjunct to this advice is to avoid pushing your host into a corner. Even if he didn't start out being confrontational, if you insist on "winning" the argument, you will most likely lose for the reasons cited above. Hosts don't like to be made to look wrong, even though some should be quite familiar with the situation. Avoid sounding as though you are smarter or lecturing. You might couch your information by quoting sources or saying, "I just read the other day..." or, "Did you see the article that said...?"

While the urge may arise to call someone a groundless narcissist, try to sublimate the feeling. There is an old adage about not tangling with the guy who buys ink by the barrel, which can also be applied to whomever controls the microphone. Again, unless you're hungry for combat, it's generally best to avoid these types of programs altogether.

Some programs attract polemicists who can be argumentative and boring. Try to listen to a program to ensure that it has a format to your liking. Get a sense of the callers. Be clear that the program will be beneficial, or at least not harmful.

*   *   *   *   *   *

A different approach should be taken if the program has a debate format. You have a point of view and want to share it. Don't worry about giving voice to others' views just to be fair. Let the other guests make their own points. If the host is interviewing you in order to knock you and/or your beliefs down, let him stake out his own positions. That said, you may sometimes want to raise expected arguments against your positions before the opponents do if you think you can effectively undercut them. For example, "It is said that my plan can't work because of this that and the other thing, but that's not true and here's why."

If you are defending a position or charging against one, it is best to consider the soft points in your argument and the strong points in any possible counter arguments. The less you are prepared, the more likely you are to be caught and revealed as uninformed. It is very important in a debate situation to define yourself and your positions before your opponent can. If you are put on the defensive, you can spend the whole event trying to dig yourself out of a hole.

Remember, too, that you don't always have to rebut an argument against your position. Such arguments are often transparent or specious. The audience will get it without your having to say something. Also, the host may jump in and add a comment. In most situations, the more anxious you seem, the less credible your position may appear. When the audience views you as thoughtful and desiring to get to the truth, rather than just clinging to your ideas, your position will have more credence.

Another thing to keep in mind is the way in which you interact with the hosts or reporters. This should go without saying, but never intentionally insult them or make them feel stupid for asking a question. They ask questions because they want answers or clarification. You may have spent the last thirty years studying the reproductive habits of banana slugs in a remote redwood forest of Humboldt County, but the chances of the reporter you're speaking with having any knowledge about this particular subject is slim. If you make them feel inadequate, you could be rewarded with half-hearted to downright nasty coverage.

Some interviewers, particularly broadcasters, get off on their guests saying their name. It's a curious kind of stroke that they think enhances their position with their listeners. Indeed, there is something personal about saying, "Yes, Fred" and "Good question, Fred," and, "I'm glad you asked that question, Fred," but it can sound gratuitous when it is over-used.

Perhaps this needn't be said, but the better an interviewer feels about the interviewee, the more likely he will be to cut his guest some slack. Even the most professional interviewer is going to, perhaps just subconsciously, treat his guest a little better than if he has no feelings or downright dislikes the person. Don't toady up to the interviewer, but don't avoid amicability.

*   *   *   *   *   *

Before you start an interview – before you enter the studio, before you get out of your car, for that matter – be sure to turn off your cell phone, pager, and anything else that might beep or buzz or ring. Indeed, don't even carry noise-making devices into the building. Your best answer might be rendered unintelligible because your phone rang at just the wrong moment.

When you're doing a television interview, try to choose a chair that doesn't swivel. If that's your only option, lock it and yourself against the desk. Swiveling chairs often make noise and create distractions, and show the seated person as nervous. Sit up straight, on the front part of the chair. Clasp your hands loosely in your lap. If you are using notes, try to keep your hands still until you need them for something. Don't touch your face. Don't scratch. And keep your head straight; many people tend to cock their heads slightly to one side or the other.

In a television interview, do not look at the camera, other people on the set, or the audience. Look directly at the host, since it's his show and it's up to him to lead.

Also, you never have to worry about where to look since he's the one you are conversing with. Lastly, keeping your eye on the interviewer is advantageous since his body language will provide non-verbal cues.

You may not like the idea of wearing make-up, but if your interview will last more than a minute consider applying a little foundation or "pancake" make-up. It dulls the shine. In our society, shiny faces are a negative. At the very least, wipe your face, particularly around your nose and eyes and inside your ears. (If you are a reporter, it's not a bad idea to carry around a compact for such circumstances, for you or your interviewee.)

Also, provide your personal information on a five-by-eight card, printed in upper and lower case. The information should include your name – with a pronunciation key, if there is ANY question – book title, if that's what the interview is about, company and position, your next appearance, primary contact information, and website, if applicable. Secondary contact information should also be on the card in smaller type, or away from the primary; for example, an agent's name, phone number, mailing address.

Make a second card for yourself. Everyone who has done a lot of interviews will own up to having forgotten the most basic information – even their own names, literally, or names of their books – albeit usually so briefly that it's not noticed. But why risk it? Put the card in front of you. It will also be a reminder to plug your book or website.

Another thing to jot down is information about the

particular interview. This is vital for authors on book tours who might do so many interviews that they forget where they are or to whom they are speaking. Have the reporter's or host's name, the name of the broadcast or newspaper, the city, the station's call letters (and frequency), and the station's call-in line on that card in front of you.

*   *   *   *   *   *

The better you know your story, the easier it is to tell. There are also many different ways to tell it, and which you choose should be based on several factors:

-- How well you know the topic

-- Your audience

-- How knowledgeable they are

-- Time constraints

Of course you should know your subject but you should also focus on the reason for doing each interview. This may seem obvious, but some people who find themselves doing multiple interviews sometimes forget why they are doing them. This is common with authors whose publicists send them on book tours, or celebrities who might do dozens of interviews in a single day.

The stories are usually the same – a new book, film, recording, political campaign – but the audiences can be very different. For example, a politician will be speaking to a different audience on the local and national levels. What is the audience's context? What are their interests? How will they receive the information that you are there to deliver?

The purpose of an interview is to communicate, so you need to know your audience beforehand, and the members' level of understanding. For example, if you are an economist and have four minutes to discuss a panic sale of Pyongyang Electric Company futures on the Tripoli Overnight Index, you better hope the only people listening have been avidly watching the story unfold so they can digest everything you say.

Similarly, if you start discussing lagging and leading economic indicators, you are going to see glazed eyeballs from here to Sunday unless your listeners are business forecasters. For generic audiences, simply say that you're watching signs for an improved economy. On the other hand, if the program is airing on a college radio station, and you are speaking about U.S. foreign policies in Africa, you could have room with the audience to toss in some anecdotes and nuance.

The point is, you will be able to tell your story from various angles and provide different perspectives based on how well you know the facts. You can push your audience, or put them to sleep, and there's often a lot of room in between to customize your presentation.

Also, keep in mind the time constraints involved in different media. A magazine with a 45-day publication lead time should be handled differently from a daily newspaper coming out tomorrow, or a blogger who will have your words on-line minutes after they leave your mouth.

While TV and radio are limited by time, print is limited by space. Again, outline the main points you want to make before speaking with the reporter to ensure that the most important information makes it into the story.

Generally, you should consider the maxim: "Tell 'em what you're gonna tell 'em, Tell 'em, then Tell 'em what you told 'em." Don't be obvious about restating your points, but make sure that you've made them clearly, and in order, so as to eliminate any potential for confusion. The more sophisticated the audience, the less you have to repeat.

You will naturally be expected to know the answers to most of the questions the interviewer asks. Say "I don't know" when you don't know the answer to a question, rather than making something up. That's a rule that shouldn't be broken.

On the other hand, that answer gets old very quickly. If you don't have all the information, make that clear to the interviewer beforehand if you can. If he asks questions outside your area of expertise, be honest and say, "That's not in my field" or, "I could recommend an expert to answer that question." But don't be dragged into making even an educated guess, because if that guess turns out to be wrong, your credibility on other issues that you do know will be undermined.

Similarly, don't try to fake it if you don't understand the question. It could be valid, just poorly worded. If you attempt to answer the question without completely understanding it, you could confuse the audience or look like a fool. Ask the host to repeat or rephrase it, or try something like, "Are you asking me...?"

You shouldn't guess what the interviewer is trying to get at if the question is convoluted or rambling. Deal directly with the questions. That's how the audience is tracking the interview.

Sometimes there is a white elephant in the middle of the living room, and everyone knows it. You are often better off going straight to the issue with, "Of course, your listeners want to know about..." But generally, follow the questions closely and answer them simply. If there is a problem with the direction the questioner is taking, try to head him off at the pass with a response like, "Do you want to know about...?" If the interviewer is being hostile, you might say, "I want your listeners to understand that..."

If you don't know an answer or don't have an opinion, just say so. If you don't have the information, apologize and either offer to find the information, reference a website, or say where it can be found. The more you sound like you are trying to sate the listeners' need to know, the more appreciative – and, if need be, sympathetic – they will be.

Another thing to keep in mind is that humor is a marvelous and grievously underused tool. No, it's not about telling jokes, although occasionally telling a funny story that makes a point can be useful. But making light of certain matters or dropping in a self-deprecating remark can show humility and grace. Using humor successfully requires a sense of timing; you don't want to experiment with it during a live interview. It can also sound good to laugh. Some people don't have a good laugh, however, and even those who do, their laugh sometimes doesn't sound good on the air.

*   *   *   *   *   *

There are different venues where you might try to tell your story. It might be to a jury. Or to your wife as she's feeding the children. Or on an evangelical Christian radio call-in show. This is why you need to understand all of the circumstances of your explication, e.g., what are the main points to inform which audience and how will they arrive there. When determining the answers to these issues, it is often best practice to start with a foundation. For instance, to think of how you would explain something complex to a local general assignment reporter who will need the basics, and in order.

The better you know your story, the easier it is to tell. The way you tell your story is based on how much time you have, who is your audience and what knowledge they already (presumably) have, and who and how well-informed is your interviewer. The point is, the more familiar you are with the facts, the more angles you can pursue, the more perspectives you can provide. You can push your audience, or put them to sleep, and there's often a lot of room in between to customize your presentation.

*   *   *   *   *   *

You can win a sawbuck every time. Bet someone he doesn't know the end of the phrase "A picture is worth...." They will always say "a thousand words" and they will be wrong. Look it up in Bartlett's. The ancient Chinese expression says a picture is worth ten thousand words. This underscores the significance we place on our visual sense.

We know that the more attractive people get the jobs

and a choice of dates on Saturday night. That's not going to change. But there are many aspects to being attractive, starting with making the best with what you have. Avoid cover-ups or trying to appear to be someone you are not. The closest you can look to who you are, the more the audience will trust you.

While preparing for a TV interview or photo shoot, make sure that how you look is consistent with how you sound – both in your tone of voice and your choice of words. Consistency neither has to be, nor should be, boring. But you don't want to distract your viewers or listeners from your words with how you look. Someone spouting macroeconomics shouldn't show up for the interview topless or sporting a pink Mohawk.

A local paper referred to a 2006 Congressional candidate who used to play rock music as a "punk rocker," and featured an old photo of him. You can imagine how the voters reacted to this. He would have been better off supplying the paper with a current photograph. If you are asked to supply photos of yourself, make sure they are appropriate for the content. Since you control the content, choose flattering images that show you in engaging situations. The best shots are usually candid, because they allow the viewer to look at you without you looking back posed.

(Consider this metaphor. You're playing right field in a softball game. If the ball is hit directly toward you, it can be difficult to judge how hard it was hit; whether it will fall short or is headed over your head. If the ball is hit on a slight angel, you have more perspective on it. You can see if you'll have to go in or back to catch it. Similarly with photographs, if the subject is looking away, the viewer can size him up on an angle.)

Almost all photographers now use digital cameras. If you're posing for a photo, say for the business page, ask the photographer to let you see the picture after it's been taken. That way you can get a preview before it's splashed on the front page or posted on the Internet.

*   *   *   *   *   *

If you are doing an interview outside of a studio, avoid speaker-phones and cell phones. Even when you're not moving around, the quality of your voice will be inferior with such devices. The better the quality of the connection, the less effort it takes the listeners to understand what you are saying. Find a place where you won't be interrupted, where there are no other phones ringing, and where the ambient noise won't detract from how you sound.

If you are doing interviews from your home or office on a regular basis, get a separate phone line to avoid bleeding from other lines in the system; and no extra features like call waiting that might insert a tone. It's also a good idea to invest in a high-quality telephone; the cheap ones don't provide good audio quality. This is particularly important if you are conducting long distance interviews where the quality of the phone line can make the difference between intelligent and unintelligible.

*   *   *   *   *   *

Reporters aren't necessarily lazier than other professionals, but like other professionals, the easier you make their jobs, the more likely they are to look upon you favorably in their report. So they will appreciate it when you say whatever you have to say as concisely as possible. Some interviewees have a tendency to run sentences together without completing their original thoughts. This can aggravate editors who are looking for a quick sound bite. On the other hand, answering questions with a simple "yes" or "no" or short phrases doesn't produce a usable piece of interview.

When answering questions, speak in complete sentences – especially when you are doing a broadcast interview that will or might be edited later, or with a print reporter, who will definitely edit your responses. As a simple example, if the reporter asks about your favorite vacation spots and you respond with, "Monterey, London and Boston," the reporter's question will have to be used before your answer to set it up, or kill your voice and write it into the voice-over. But if you say, "My favorite vacation spots are Monterey, London and Boston," it will be much easier to fit into a report. You can then take a short beat and add, "And let me tell you why."

When reporters are working on deadline and don't have time to call back for clarification, they will usually make the best sense they can out of whatever you said. So, if you don't want to be misquoted or have something taken out of context, the more you have said in complete sentences, the less likelihood there will be for misunderstanding.

Frequently you will have a longer answer than the reporter might want to air, but it all needs to be said. To avoid being edited you might begin with, "Lance, there are three critical aspects to this problem your viewers need to understand." And then follow up immediately with "First, the man they are trying has an air-tight alibi. Second, he couldn't have driven the getaway car because he is blind. And third, the witnesses identified the district attorney as the person who fired the shots." That makes it tough to cut your answer. Especially if you are on camera and you tick off the reasons on your fingers.

In broadcast interviews you also have the option of keeping your voice up at the end of a sentence if you haven't completed your thought. Editors are less likely to clip you prematurely.

You don't want to frustrate your audience with incomplete information or information that is not in some easily absorbable sequence. This is obviously more of a challenge when you are discussing more complex issues, because most people will hear what you have to say only once and either can't or won't play it back. Guide the audience. Enumerate a series of points as you did with Lance above or Tell 'em what you're gonna tell 'em first so that they will understand where you are going before you actually get to the heart of the issue.

This is important when their ability to understand your story depends on their knowledge of a secondary issue. For instance, if you were talking about the quagmire in Iraq, and comparing it to what happened to the U.S. in Vietnam, first you would give a brief outline of how the U.S. got entangled in Southeast Asia. Then you would describe the situation in Iraq. And finally, if necessary, you would draw the comparisons.

*   *   *   *   *   *

Authors used to grant interviews so they could share the information in their books in a more intimate forum. The audience was often filled with fans who had read their previous books and wanted to get to know the author on a more personal level. At the end of the interview, some liked what they heard and bought a copy, while others were glad they didn't waste their money.

But a large percentage of authors are now hawking their books through the interview process. It's a big business, and so important to sales that some publishers will pass on a good book written by an author who doesn't interview well. (Well, hey, they've replaced their editors with public relations people.)

Those authors who wind up on book publicity tours rarely have anything good to say about the experience. Rarely will one of the scores of interviewers have read, or even opened, the book. He often hasn't even read the press information that provides background about the author, details about the book, and other useful information. But even in the worst circumstances, when confronted with the host's ignorance of everything about the author and his book, the author should never tell the host to, Go read the book!. It can happen when frustration levels rise. Unfortunately, the inference by the audience is that the host didn't think the book was worth his time to read it; and that suggests that the audience hasn't the time either.

The truth is that professional interviewers often don't have the time to read every guest's book. If you are hosting a two-hour daily talk show, you are likely to be talking with at least four authors a week, maybe twice that many depending on how many guests you interview in those two hours. Even Evelyn Wood wouldn't be expected to read four books a week.

Sometimes hosts find themselves too busy to do any research at all; some don't even get the author's name or book title right. In fairness, it's not always their fault. A guest could drop out at the last minute and an author could be called to fill the empty slot, or a producer could connect with the wrong person with the same name. There are plenty of legitimate excuses for a talk show host not to be familiar with a guest, his work or even his subject. The results can be quite entertaining, though not for the host.

Having the guest prep the host for the interview may seem like a specious idea, but it ain't no more. Back in the old days, interviewees would rarely have the temerity to ask to see or hear the questions beforehand. They were even more unlikely to suggest what the questions should be. But many public relations representatives and publishers now send press kits replete with "sample" questions prior to the interview.

Some interviewers will then read off the questions in order. Whether this is done out of laziness or unfamiliarity with the material, you the author/interviewee should respond as though you were hearing the questions for the first time, and that they prompted you to deliver a thoughtful response. After all, you're there to answer the questions and to pique the audience's interest.

In cases where you find yourself sitting across from someone who is supposed to be asking questions about your book, only to discover he knows virtually nothing about it – take the proverbial reins of the interview, without appearing to do so. It's important that you be subtle about this, because not only might you upset the interviewer, but also the audience, which has its own listening habits.

You can be very obvious with the unprepared host by saying such things as, "I bet you wanted to know..." or more subtle with, "I'm sure your listeners are waiting to hear about..." If you want positive results, do this in a light and encouraging tone. Complete sentences are even more important in these situations, as is telling your story in order, because you're carrying the ball alone. But because it's your book – your story – and you are already familiar with the subject matter, you should be able to lead the interview, and enjoy it.

Start at the beginning with the most obvious questions the audience will want answered and move on to the next, relating one to another. Some interviewers will be grateful; others won't realize what has happened. Most interviewers will be somewhere in between. If you do your part, they will often show up sometime in the middle. Give them a lead like, "People ask me why I didn't just take up quilting," and even the most un-conscious interviewer will come back with, "And why didn't you?"

*   *   *   *   *   *

When you come to the point of winding up the interview, make sure that you give the audience a way to get more information, e.g., a website. Also, thank the interviewer for the opportunity to share your ideas with his listeners. And if you promised any material, such as a few give-away books to use in station promotions, for example, make sure to deliver them quickly, and with the thank-you card as the cover.

Any time you do a serious interview – not the quickie sound bite kind, but those that took some time to set up or produce – send a thank-you note, especially if the host did his homework and maintained a lively dialogue.

Depending on the situation, consider keeping the interviewer updated on your developments. It might be appropriate to ask if you can include his e-mail address on your mailing list.

*   *   *   *   *   *

Whether doing the interview for print or broadcast, always be conscious of the clock. This is important on several levels. First, the less you "dump" on the interviewer the more attention will be focused on what you provide. Second, the interviewer will likely (if unconsciously) present your story in a better light if you respect his time. And third, the less time you spend promoting your product or ideas, the more time you'll have left for answering more questions.

For live broadcasts, the clock is the ultimate diviner of how much time is available and on what schedule. There are a certain number of minutes devoted to opens and closes, commercials, news headlines, and bumpers. It says when the program starts, when the interviewer must interrupt the conversation for words from the sponsors. It tells you when your time is up.

On commercial broadcasts, an interview segment might run only four minutes. Or you might be told that you have the second half hour of a program, and the actual interviewing might run eighteen minutes, depending on the other elements that are part of the format. And those eighteen minutes might be broken into three or four segments. If you turn out to be a bore, you might be dumped early. If you make a great guest, they may extend you, but more likely you will be asked to return (because other people are already booked in).

Some interviews are taped in pattern; that is, they are recorded as if they were live, with an open, breaks for commercials, and a close. Even though they are pre-recorded, because they are in pattern, they are rarely edited. Other feature interviews are conducted open-ended and then edited to conform to time. It is in this latter format that an interviewee generally has the most latitude in delivering his information.

The more you are able to tell your story in concise pieces, the easier will be the editing later. Elements that have a beginning, a middle, and an end will be obvious choices to remain in the report. Also, those accounts that are easiest for the audience to follow will likely to be included. These criteria are suggested on top of what is truly important to the audience. And to what makes the interviewer look good, if it comes to that.

So however the interview is structured, you want to know approximately how much time you'll have to tell your story – all that you want to deliver and the extra pieces. You'll also want to leave time for questions. Before you ever enter a studio you should have good idea how long it will take you to deliver each piece of your story, so you won't try to shoe-horn a six minute item into a three-minute hole. You'll know how long it will take to deliver your pieces, and still leave room for the host to follow up with questions.

Some conversations can be reasonably interrupted with commercial breaks, but some suffer. If you do have to stop for a break, make sure you remind the audience what you were discussing before the interruption.

Don't be a slave to the clock. Have some faith in the interviewer to manage the time of his program properly. But when you walk into a studio, see if there is a production or wall clock in your purview. If not, see if you can make your watch visible easily. But be discreet about looking at either; if the host notices you looking at it, he will not only feel disconcerted – perhaps feel that you are being rude – and he may also feel pushed off his schedule.

Time goes by surprisingly quickly once the interview starts. Watching the allotted number of minutes tick down second by second causes some people to rush through their points, while others quickly figure out how to effectively convey their messages. As a general rule, there is never as much time as you think there is for your purposes. The more experience you have doing interviews, the better you'll become at using the available time to your best advantage. You will also be able to more accurately size up the interviewer, his predilections, style and direction.

And this...the better interviewee you make – the better the interview you create from the host's perspective – the more likely you are to be invited back.

* * * * * *

Most of broadcasting today is managed by a computer. The broadcast schedule is run by the computer on the basis of the actual time of day. It will go to the news source at the top of the hour, for instance, then play a two minute commercial, and turn on the host's microphone at six minutes past the hour. The computer schedule can be manipulated in some cases, but most on-air people have learned not to mess with it.

Each program has its own schedule of content and commercials programmed into the computer. In broadcast lingo, that program schedule or format is referred to as the clock. The clock includes all of the scheduled times in the broadcast, from on to off with all of the breaks and program times in between. Many broadcasts with set clocks have audio bumpers which start a certain time before the commercial automatically begins to play. These bumpers are designed to give the host a warning that he needs to wrap up his thoughts in a half-minute or less. It is a buffer time that may run thirty seconds, during which the host will break off from the interview and ease into the commercial. They also signal affiliated stations that the commercial break is coming, in case they are going to insert a local message. If you are talking when that music starts, you should try to finish your thought in half that time to give the host the time to make a smooth transition.

Some hosts, believing it helps them to keep control, don't explain the bumpers to their interviewees. The smart hosts do, however, because they know that the cooperative guest will wind down quickly and give the host the time to make a clean break. The smart ones understand that the smoother the broadcast, the better they all sound. Does it need to be said? Don't try to fill the bumper time. It's not your show. You're the guest.

If a thought hasn't been concluded before the commercial plays – if you have to interrupt a story – you probably want to conclude it afterwards. The host may say before the break, "Let's take that up when we come back" but there's a good chance that neither of you will remember by the time the commercials finish playing. Especially these days, when the commercial breaks stretch interminably.

It is therefore not a bad idea to keep track of what is being discussed. You should come into the interview with a prioritized list of points you want to make, and cross them off as they are being covered. A corollary to that is to track what is being discussed so when you are interrupted by a commercial break or the news, you can reprise that thought. Write a note to yourself so you remember what it was you were talking about and where to pick up again.

If would be nice if the interviewer came back with, "As we were saying before the break …," but they often use the breaks to use the restroom or talk with their producers. The commercial ends, the interviewer says, "We're back …," and you can hear in his voice or see in his eyes that he barely recalls what day it is. If you have jotted down a note about what you were discussing when you entered the break, you can come back with, "Harry, we were talking about the problem of the broadcasting lobby …"

The more familiar you are with your story and the

program's clock, the more easily you can direct the conversation and ensure that all of your points are made in a logical order. You don't want to appear to be challenging the host for control of "his" broadcast. But if you are dealing with someone who is lost in the interview or hasn't done his homework, you can help to steer the interview to interesting aspects of your story that will serve both your needs.

*   *   *   *   *   *

Remember to enunciate. Speak about ten percent more slowly than you would in person. Wait until the host (or caller or another guest) has finished talking before you begin speaking again. It's not only polite, but more effective. T. S. Eliot observed, "Except for the point, the still point, there would be no dance, and there is only the dance." Moments of silence are punctuation. They give the listeners the opportunity to reset their receptors for a different speaker.

Also, remember to keep your voice level up. Many people have a tendency to drop their voices at the end of a sentence, so that their last words are lost. This is extremely frustrating for both the audience and host during an interview situation. Keeping your voice up is even more important when you are conducting an interview by telephone, since the telephone and the telephone lines seem to bend in the direction of the voice. If you have ever seen the waveform display of an interview, especially one conducted by phone, you will invariably see a decline – sometimes substantial – at the end of comments by a less-experienced speaker.

Most of us have a tendency to use filler words like

"um," "er," "well," and "like" as place-holders. The occasional space-filling sound is part of normal conversation, but these words are now being used with mindless and meaningless frequency. If you don't know what you want to say, let others do the talking. Using, "Well," to begin a sentence is frequently a starter for beginning a conversation, but it can be annoying if it precedes every sentence.

A flip side of this issue is to avoid long pauses. It's fine for people to think before they speak, but if you are doing a radio interview, long pauses can raise questions in the listeners' minds: Did the station go off the air? Did the tape break? You'd be surprised how long even a short silence can sound.

If you get lost in your thoughts or are searching for an example to illustrate a concept, ask to revisit the subject later. If the host seems lost, break in with, "I wonder, Roger, if your listeners would be interested in knowing about how much the guy spent at Tiffany's..."

*   *   *   *   *   *

Don't worry about how "professional" you sound. If you know what you're talking about, the professionalism will take care of itself. In fact, just about anyone who doesn't have regular practice with public speaking can sound inexperienced in an interview. In many instances, that is only appropriate; a passerby who witnesses a traffic accident is not expected to sound like an experienced on-air reporter at the scene.

If you stay in your role as the tyro performer – as the person from whom the information is being extracted – the audience will stay with you. Or at least as long as you don't either confuse or bore them. If you are talking about a subject that is unfamiliar to most people, give them the big picture first, and if you have the time, then get into the specifics. Don't talk down to the audience. Explain what needs to be made clear. Explain in a way that you would to the man who is going to be your father-in-law, i.e., with respect and a desire to inform. Be selective about how much you feed your listeners; they're only going to give you a few minutes to prove you are worth their attention.

In most cases, time constraints will limit you to making no more than five points. They should be headlined and quickly linked to the main topic. You don't want to say, "It all comes back to ..." more than once or twice, but that should be your thinking.

The brilliant Canadian writer Robertson Davis had a character say, "I always preferred metaphor to reason." When you are educating an audience, it is always more effective to provide both ideas and examples – especially when you are talking about concepts that aren't easily grasped with words alone. It's similar to giving directions. You might say to follow this road a mile and then turn right, but if you add that there's a gas station on the corner, the directions will be ever more useful.

Though tuned into your interview, many listeners are doing something else, such as driving or cooking dinner. Because their attention is thus split, it is all the more important that you tell your story clearly, so they can absorb the salient facts while avoiding pedestrians or burning the roast. By selecting the most important information and delivering it in an easily understandable way, you are doing some of their thinking for the listeners. This is fine as long as you're not seen as manipulative or trying to deceive. So if you are guiding the listeners' understanding, stay on topic, be clear and accurate, and don't sound like a sales person.

*　　*　　*　　*　　*　　*

The more original you are in your thinking and presentation the more likely you are to engage and hold the audience. Not that you should deliberately sound bizarre; rather, you should avoid sounding common. For instance, you should remove from your lexicon phrases like "To tell the truth" and "To be perfectly frank" which raise the issue of whether you're being perfectly candid otherwise. Also, try not to say "At the end of the day" which was rated the most frequently over-used phrase in a recent study. Or "When all is said and done" because all is never said and few are rarely done.

Civility

On whichever side of the microphone you stand, you always have the right to demand civility of the other person. If an agreement has been made to have an interview, then one person has to agree to ask the questions and the other to answer them. If the accord breaks apart somewhere in the middle, excuse yourself, but don't put up with abuse unless you knew it was coming, e.g., you accepted a date with someone like Bill O'Reilly.

Sometimes it is necessary for the interviewee to interrupt his host such as when the questioner goes on a tangent based on an incorrect presumption and takes it too far. Or perhaps you realize that you misstated something and need to correct it immediately to avoid the interviewer launching into an endless extrapolation on the wrong answer. When you must interrupt, always say, "Excuse me," and remain silent until the host finishes speaking.

If you are interrupted by your interviewer, stop talking. When you both are speaking, all that comes through the radio is garble. On television it looks like a hen fight.

Don't speak again until the host has stopped talking. If it happens again, wait again. If he has to prompt you to speak this time, you might say, "I wanted to make sure that you were finished." And if it happens yet again, wait to be prompted again and say, "I wanted you to have the opportunity to complete your thought." If you are interrupted a fifth time, it may be time to say "Thank you," and leave.

*　*　*　*　*　*

Mike Wallace of *Sixty Minutes* and Geraldo Rivera were among the most egregious of ambush interviewers. The former often showed discretion, something to which the latter seemed particularly adverse. Somewhere in between is where a good reporter/interviewer is likely to find the most maneuvering room. Yes, ambush interviews are appropriate when someone who owes a public explanation is refusing to provide it. Most times.

No, it is not right to invade a person's privacy when the matter is personal and shouldn't be made public. The importance of the story and the interview dictate how far you might reach. Shooting through the windows of a home should be off limits, so should anywhere else that a person might reasonably expect privacy.

Also, the paparazzi-style coverage of celebrities hoping to enjoy privacy in public is often well over the top of what should be acceptable. Interrupting a target's dinner to ask questions is usually inappropriate, though if you happen on someone you really want to interview, you might say, "Excuse me, I know this is not the place, but might I please set up an appointment to speak with you?" If the response is yes, grand, do it. If it is hostile, withdraw politely.

There are two reasons for respecting a person's privacy, their right to it, and how you look invading it. There is a school of reality coverage that suggests that anyone is fair game at any time. Harassing people, interrupting what might be construed as their personal lives may seem bold to some, but often it is just cheesy, and it looks it.

*   *   *   *   *   *

What are you to do if the person you are interviewing says something especially candid while you are re-cording an interview, and later asks you not to use it? Is the material still fair game, or should you respect their wishes and withhold it? That has to depend on the specific circumstances. The bottom line is, if you have it on tape after they were aware you were recording you can use it. But that's not always appropriate. If it was a personal revelation that doesn't advance the cov-erage, it should probably come out. If it was impor-tantly revelatory to the character of the person – he screamed at an aide – then if should probably stay in. If something is acquired honestly, exercise due discretion as to whether or not it's airing would be of significant – not prurient – interest to the audience.

*   *   *   *   *   *

Interruptions are frequent on broadcast programs that are based on confrontation. Some hosts haven't the intellect to appeal on the basis of substance. Jerry Springer would stage full-scale brawls on his set. As well-informed as he seems to be, Bill O'Reilly stoops to attracting viewers by insulting his guests. The best advice for you is to avoid such programs, but if you do find yourself in a situation that has suddenly turned hostile, you can avoid falling into a deeper hole by remaining calm yourself.

If you find yourself in this situation, slow down the pace. Pause, take a deep breath, and answer thoughtfully. If the heat rises when you are working with an otherwise-honest interviewer, you can say something like, "This is a difficult area for me..."

With a more obtuse questioner, you can then try "That's not what I came here to talk about," or "I don't think your listeners are interested in that." Such responses challenge the host but give him room to resume the normal course of the interview. It certainly makes you look better to the audience than if you come out with, "That's none of your business."

Another suggestion for when the pace gets beyond what is comfortable – before an interview and/or during it – is to touch your belly, and take a slow, quiet breath deep into your center. The Japanese word *hara* refers to your midpoint, about an inch and a half below your navel. Subtly touching your hara and breathing into it (figuratively) can lower the noise level in your head and give you the opportunity to focus on what you want to convey.

Sound Enhancing Tips

Hare are some suggestions for how to make your interviews sound better.

If you have trouble understanding audio in the editing room, your viewers or listeners are more than likely to miss it entirely. This can be very frustrating when you're cutting a sound bite and you hear exactly what you want, but only after you play it three or four times. Apply this criterion strictly: If you are selecting a cut from an interview you conducted yourself and it isn't clear the first time you play the tape back, alarm bells should go off.

Working in television, one trick to help your viewers better understand someone who is going to speak on camera, perhaps not very intelligibly, is to show that person speaking before you have him deliver the sound cut. Using such an establishing shot creates a degree of familiarity with the person before the viewer has to listen to him speak.

Another suggestion: Give the person time to speak. Any sound cut shorter than ten seconds, especially the first time that person speaks, is going to strain the viewers' ability to contextualize the new voice. Obvious exceptions include hearing a person speaking a second or third time, and chants, screams and other brief exclamations. Considering the attention span and subliminal expectations of the average viewer, eighteen seconds seems to be the optimum length for a basic sound cut.

This goes against the grain for a lot of today's news directors, who favor staccato editing with short sound cuts. They object to "talking-heads" on principle, and will rant and rave about their reporters not having the brains to realize that television is a visual medium. Sometimes they have a point, but usually they have been reading too much "expert" research or listening to consultants, neither of which usually consider journalism to be an important factor in television news. If you don't need the job, or already have another one lined up, you might remind that news director that people like Ted Koppel, Barbara Walters and Mike Wallace have found considerable success in using talking-heads.

Sometimes, if the sound is particularly crucial to your story, you can run sub-titles below it. Sometimes. In the late '70s, when I was producing news for ABC, Harry Reasoner conducted a long-distance interview with Leon Spinks, the day after the boxer had beaten Muhammad Ali. A camera was set up in Reasoner's office, and another was set up on Spinks in a hotel room in Las Vegas. The two spoke over the telephone. The tape from Las Vegas was then to be sent by satellite to New York, where I would edit the pieces together.

I listened in on a telephone extension so that I could

take notes on both sides of the conversation. But I could understand very little of what Spinks said and became very worried. After the short conversation, which Reasoner somehow understood without difficulty, I expressed my concerns to Av Westin, the executive producer of the ABC Evening News. He said people would be able to understand because they could watch Spinks' lips move. That made sense.

The alternative was to use sub-titles, but that would have elicited attacks from people who would suggest we were mocking Spinks because he was black. It was not an unreasonable concern on our part, even in those days when political correctness had not gone as far overboard as it has today. But with Westin's mollification in my mind, I headed for the tape room.

He was right, it was easier, but it was still difficult to fully understand Spinks. As it turned out, there was enough video that was at least marginal so that we could play it without sub-titles. But a good percentage of the audience probably couldn't understand him and had to infer most of what they did grok from Reasoner's questions and responses.

*   *   *   *   *   *

Many top crews will record room tone after an interview in a seemingly quiet room, and when used under set-up shots or voice-over bridges, the recording can enhance the overall quality of the report.

Even when you are recording a simple interview, where the sound should be easy to control, take the time to set up correctly. Pushing a microphone in the general direction of the guest's mouth may be enough in some situations, but the quality of the audio can often be muddled unless the microphone is properly positioned and held still. Also, a windscreen can make the difference between intelligible or not.

Lavaliers – The small, clip-on microphones usually attached to a collar or shirt front – are usually used in studios and other controlled situations, such as sit-down interviews. Interviewees inexperienced at being interviewed on television frequently make the mistake of brushing the mic with their hands or arms, or creating noise by rustling their clothing. Watch out, too, for necklaces and neckties, which can clatter, rustle, or scratch at the wrong moment. Save time, tape and effort by placing the microphone out of the way as much as possible, and instructing the guest to avoid touching it. If you see the person brush it, wait until he has finished his answer, then check your tape to make sure the answer is usable.

Hand-held - It's microphone looks like a large lollipop with a thick stem. Hand-helds are useful in stand-uppers or in an unstructured location interview. One example would be when the reporter needs to control who is speaking, such as eyewitness accounts of a fire from a group of bystanders. Make sure that you are on the same page with whoever is recording the sound as far as where to position the microphone and how close it should be.

Shotgun - This mic looks like a baton and is usually protected by a foam windscreen. Shotguns – which come in sizes ranging from eight inches to a couple of feet – are used in directional work, pointed at the sound source. Shotguns are very useful in crowd scenes, like a walking news conference, and for recording a stand-upper or an interview when the reporter needs to keep his hands free.

Table microphone - It's the kind you see sitting on a desk in front of people. They aren't used in news that much anymore, except to record group interviews, because lavaliers are usually more functional.

Boom - This microphone is used in studios and lowered from above the speaker or speakers. The boom is a long pole with a swivel control on the end that allows the mic to be held above the camera shot, and pointed directly toward the speaker.

Parabolic - A long-distance, directional microphone that looks like a microwave dish. Except in spy movies, it's rarely used to record an interview unless it is shot on a staged set with outside sound protection. It is often used at sporting events to pick up the sound athletes make on the field.

In addition to knowing about microphones, you also might come across these two terms for earpieces – IFB and SAR – but probably not. This is only being inserted here because it was teased at the top of the book. IFB stands for interrupted feedback. It is a signal from the studio to the reporter in the field which feeds program that can be interrupted with instruction by the director or the producer. SAR stands for selected audio return, and it means certain sound is fed back to a non-reporter type in a remote location needing to hear sound from the studio. For instance, the audio from an anchor in the studio in New York talking with a guest interviewee in Death Valley.

Television Tips

In a studio situation, position your guests far enough from the camera so that if they gesture or cross their legs, the motion doesn't dominate the picture or get cut off by the frame. A cameraman will sometimes go in tight on a face, and if the person suddenly moves, he'll be out of the frame. Inform your cameraman how you want the shots framed so that he knows whether to stay wide or go tight.

The interviewee should be facing the interviewer, not the camera, but should be shot more or less head-on, probably within fifteen degrees of center whenever possible. It is much easier for the audience to understand a person – both verbally and non-verbally – when the interviewee's face is open to them. If you are being interviewed and the camera lens is at too great an angle from the host, tell the host that it's difficult to address to the audience. The other option is to say nothing but simply or look back and forth every so often between the camera and the interviewer. That way you acknowledge both.

(You will rarely shoot an interview in which you want

to conceal someone's identity, but for such a situation, the cameraman should simply shoot from behind, or without any front lights to create a silhouette image.)

The visuals of a television interview aren't usually very dynamic. Unless there is considerable by-play, all the audience will usually see is the interviewee, and perhaps a two-shot with the interviewer. Therefore, subtle, visual nuances such as body language (on top of hair, make-up and clothing) become more important, as concomitantly does the content of the interview. (This obviously matters less if you are just going for a couple of short sound bites than if you are airing a 10-minute segment with one talking head, in which case many reporters will seek to cover some of the interview with relevant video.)

A stand-upper will sometimes wrap around a live interview. That is, the camera will start tight on the reporter, and after a script cue or a physical move by the reporter, the shot will widen out to include the interviewee. Then it will tighten up again on the reporter for a close. While you can offer some obvious lines like, "With us now is...," and, "Thank you...," you might instead use a body turn or have simple hand signals. Of course, make sure that the cameraman knows to look for hand signals at the appropriate time, and not through the lens since your hands will likely be out of the shot.

*   *   *   *   *   *

When setting up an interview, think about what will be a good background for the shot, i.e., reinforcing the person's identity. While producing an interview in the

Hershey Chocolate boardroom, for example, I positioned the company president in front of a wall bearing a portrait of the founder, Milton S. Hershey II. The cameraman started tight on the portrait and then pulled back to show the president in a wide shot.

*   *   *   *   *   *

Try not to conduct interviews outside in a strong breeze; even with a windscreen, the sound will suffer.

*   *   *   *   *   *

When shooting an on-the-go handheld interview, position yourself on the other side of the camera from the photographer. If he's using a right-eye viewfinder, you want to be on his right, his blind side. He can see on the left, and you can protect him on his right. If there is a second person in the crew, he should be on the other side of the photographer, similarly protecting him from unexpected low branches or jostling.

Standing on the right side of the camera, hold the microphone in your left hand. This way (1) you won't be reaching across yourself and you will have more flexibility where you hold the microphone, and (2) it will keep your right hand (usually the stronger one) free.

*   *   *   *   *   *

Before you start the actual interview, ask the cameraman to get some establishing shots, such as wide and two-shots (of you and the interviewee), and maybe some close-ups of the person's hands in his lap. And during the shooting of the interview, ask the cameraman to shoot the interviewee loosely enough to leave room for a person's name to be inserted when it airs.. Only in extended interviews should you go in very tight, for effect, and risk not providing the space for a name.

*   *   *   *   *   *

When editing your interview, you have several options for connecting two or more pieces of sound. You can cover the jump with a cutaway listening shot or a wide two-shot. Or you might prefer to tie the cuts together with a dissolve or wipe. The point is that you want to have the sound cuts together to frame an idea, and whatever you use to smooth over the edit should be designed to help the audience view the two cuts as one, with as little distraction as possible.

There are varying opinions on the use of cutaways in editing interviews. For the longest time, some television news organizations refused to allow cutaways, unless they actually shot the interview with two cameras in real time. That is certainly preferable, but few reporters have the luxury of two or more cameras to shoot an interview.

Many professionals don't think that there's anything wrong with shooting reverse listening shots if they help to make a better flow. Some do it but complain that they feel like a performer rather than a journalist. The fact is that in many instances set-up shots and cutaways do look so staged – especially the intense, nodding shots – and they can cause more of a distraction from the content of the interview than would a dissolve or wipe.

When shooting cutaways – listening shots, two-shots,

etc. – make sure that the camera is recording actual conversation. If you are conscious of the camera being on you, it will look stilted. The best route going into the edit room includes cutaways of both you and the interviewee actually listening and obviously interested. Engage your interviewee in what you are saying so that his listening set-up shot looks genuine, and when you're shooting a reverse, have the interviewee talking to you so that you are truly listening. The viewer can tell from your expression whether you are truly paying attention or just posing. It is the same difference between the forced smiles of a photo op and real conversation.

If you're going to shoot note-taking or hands-in-the-lap shots, make sure that the tone of the edited conversation during the taking of those shots matches the tone of that part of the interview for which the shots will be used. A hand moving slowly across a notebook does not fit as a cutaway in a heated dialogue.

You can also use germane b-roll (relevant video) to cover multiple edits, with the same admonition to be careful that picture and sound don't conflict. The sound cuts, like any piece of scripted voice-over, should match with the video to present a comprehensive package of information. If you do cover part of the interview, you should make every effort to start with the person on camera for at least ten seconds before you cover the voice with pictures, so that the audience is clear about who is talking. Also, come back from the pictures to the person speaking, when possible; it provides closure to the sound.

Finally on editing, it is important to remember when

cutting an interview, for a single sound cut or to lay a voice under a minute of video, that the spoken words need to be easily understandable the first time through. If you have any trouble understanding what is being said or what is meant, you can be sure you're going to lose at least part of your audience. Especially since you conducted the interview and are listening to the sound in an editing room, with a professional ear. Your audience is probably listening with half-'n-ear while eating dinner or checking their email..

*　*　*　*　*　*

When conducting a television interview, it is often useful to record with an audio copy as well. You can listen to the interview on the way back to the station and work on your script in your head.

*　*　*　*　*　*

If you're interviewing someone on his own turf, reconfirm any appointments made more than three hours earlier, if only to say you're on your way. It gives the interviewee a chance to wind up other business and prepare. Sometimes, if this will be their first experience with a professional interview, you will likely be asked if they can do anything for you, and there usually is. This can be valuable foreplay since the more involved the interviewees are in the process, the better the communication will be and the better the overall piece will turn out.

For instance, in the case of a television interview, if you want to shoot in a person's laboratory, ask that the area be set up in advance so that there isn't too much noise or background distractions. Or if it's an old building and you're going to use a lot of lights, ask if an electrician could be alerted in case any problems arise. You may also ask that certain documents or graphics be made available – an annual report or company logo on disk – which visuals you may need later in the editing room.

Another task to do while setting up is to confirm the spelling and pronunciation of the interviewee's name. Get a business card, or write everything down in your notebook, including an evening phone number, in case you need to check a fact after business hours.

When you finish the interview, make sure that the furniture is in its original position, the gaffer's tape is removed from the cornices, and the flowers are back on the table.

Mass Interviews

Polling is an abstract form of mass interviewing. The answers are pre-set, and a large number of people are being asked to choose among the answers. As much as we enjoy reading poll results, the fact is that they tend to confuse popular ideas with true public consciousness, as they fail to register ideas outside of the mainstream as reflected in the pre-selected answers. The fact that people are limited to saying yes or no to questions is deeply flawed to begin with, and especially when questions are improperly phrased.

For instance, a poll during the Robert Bork nomination process asked people if they supported President Bush's choice, Robert Bork, for the Supreme Court. Regrettably, a sizeable number of people answered "yes," not because they knew or approved of Bork, but simply because he was the President's nominee.

Consider, too, that there are a lot of people in our society who prefer to be considered – by others and themselves – mainstream, which also skews results. The problem with skewed results is that they are used to justify political positions, and that's hardly a healthy way to formulate policy.

One of the most scurrilous forms of polling is to invite viewers or website visitors to register their opinions with yes-no or multiple-choice responses to a series of questions. The results are meaningless, since there is an implication of validity when the fact is that the participants are self-chosen and can vote over and over again.

At the time of the 1980 Carter-Reagan debate – and it has become a familiar practice since – ABC invited viewers to "choose the winner" by phoning 900-numbers, one for Carter, the other for Reagan. It was a tragically-glaring example of style-over-substance reporting. Not only did it invite manipulation by either or both candidates, but the results were further undermined by the fact that each call cost fifty cents.

*   *   *   *   *   *

A common form of cheap polling is the man-on-the-street interview. Regrettably, this practice of collecting comments from people at malls or on street corners is antithetical to real news gathering. The people have no particular credentials and yet unless they are blatant in their ignorance, their opinions are "naturally" accorded some value. In our society, the very fact that someone is on television gives them certain credibility, which is why these interviews run directly counter to good journalism. Especially since, in most cases today, thoughtful, longer answers are sacrificed to pithy or entertaining remarks. Airing such interviews implies that the speakers are rational. Remember, too, that even majority opinion is fluid and often under-informed.

*   *   *   *   *   *

The press conference is a converse form of mass interview. The mass are interviewers, so to speak. What demarcates this forum from a one-on-one interview is that others share in the questioning. This provides cover if you haven't done your homework, but it also means that competing news outlets will wind up airing or printing the same quotes. Sometimes the answers they will select are to your questions, and little credit will devolve to you. This is particularly unfortunate if you have a scoop on the other reporters and have to share your knowledge before them.

Political Interviews

One of the most important forums where interviews are conducted is in our elections process. We, the People, need to know for whom we are voting in order to get the kind of government we want. Usually we don't do the interviewing ourselves, unless we are involved at the grassroots level. Mostly we leave it up to the media to ask the tough questions and to elicit clear profiles of the candidates. No wonder we're in such trouble.

Finding out where a candidate stands is one of the most important interviews that can be done. Of course, some candidates lie their way into office. Many others arrive in Washington or the statehouse or city hall to find a different reality. They discover they have fallen down Alice's rabbit hole. That the polemics of the campaign don't play in the new arena. Which makes finding the right candidate for the job all that more important, and all the more difficult.

Candidates are interviewed incessantly, sometimes one-on-one by a reporter (or in a press conference or a debate), and sometimes in meetings with groups of people whose endorsement they are trying to earn. Sometimes questions are asked in greeting lines over a handshake at an airport. This section is devoted to providing strategies that might be used effectively to better define the policies and character of those who would seek to represent us. This is not said lightly. For a government of, by, and for the people, it is ultimately up to the people to select and elect those who would govern.

If the person asking the question is at the grass roots level, and only likely to ask one question, it should be a litmus test-level question. If it is someone working for a news outlet, he should husband his time carefully so that the dozen or so questions he may get to ask in a twenty-minute interview are framed in such a way as to deliver determinant or clarifying answers.

If you represent a substantial organization, a union for example, with the potential to deliver a lot of votes, get your value from your time with the leader-wannabe. Give the candidate a lengthy list of questions and ask for a lengthy list of answers back.

*   *   *   *   *   *

It was said going into the 2004 elections that they would be the most important in American history. It was probably true at the time. In '04, the public supported President Bush, enough to leave him in the White House. However, a year after that vote, the electorate changed its mind. Indeed, if a poll had been taken in November of '05, a majority of those surveyed would likely have said they had voted for John Kerry. We are very flexible in our thinking, although our timing is often off.

Every election should be taken seriously, by both

candidates and voters. That has not been the case for much of our recent history. While we gambol around the globe pushing democracy on other nations, here in our own country, only half of those eligible actually vote. The percentage of the electorate that chooses our leaders is shamefully small, and in many situations undermines the very notion of a government of, by and, for the People. So few people now participate that our governance has fallen into the hands of special interests.

If you wonder why we suffer the ills we do, consider that some special interests are not only not suffering, but are actually benefitting from the status quo. In most such cases, policies were implemented by candidates who received campaign funds from those special interests.

It doesn't have to be this way. If better people were attracted to politics, if the people did a better job of vetting the candidates, if the media acted responsibly in informing the voters, we could eliminate the corruption and get our country back on track.

Obviously then, it is essential for the American people to know who the candidates are – both as politicians and as human beings – and what their thoughts are, and what they plan to do in office. In most cases, the substantive information is not readily available because most candidates now communicate mainly through television and radio commercials. That's because the media tend not to cover campaigns unless there is a scandal or a celebrity in the race.

Because broadcasters reap huge sums from airing those campaign commercials, they tend to discourage serious election coverage for fear that (1) they would be competing with themselves, if that makes sense, and (2) anything adverse in the coverage could induce a candidate to pull his ads from the station. Thus, most candidates get away with packaging themselves in sound bites when most of the critical issues we face today require at least a minute or two to discuss.

Any candidate who is serious about his positions, who wants the electorate to understand his policies, and what he would try to accomplish if elected, needs at least fifteen minutes in a quality interview to tell voters why they should consider him.

Most media forums won't provide that kind of time. And time is not the only issue. To have a quality interview, you need someone who knows the issues and has the temerity to ask the right questions until a satisfactory answer is provided. Most reporters lack that depth and persistence.

It's not always an easy task to interview a politician, but people shouldn't be afraid of it. Over the years, the very word "politics" has acquired a scurrilous odor, but the root is from the Greek meaning simply, "management of the community." Would that politics were simply that. Most politics today is rife with obfuscation and downright deceit, from the first campaign to retirement from public life to lobbyist or consultant.

The sleazy language of politics is derived from decades of hiding the truth from the voters, even when the truth is easier to deliver and harmless to the politician. During the late Paul Simon's Senate re-election campaign in Illinois a number of years ago, he spoke at a senior citizens home. Simon wound up taking four questions from the audience. None of them was difficult. Simon had a good record on all the issues as far as his listeners were concerned, and, it should be noted, he was a shoo-in for re-election. The Senator spent twenty minutes talking to the group through and around the issues, but he never answered the questions. He probably wasn't deliberately trying to mislead; his meandering was most likely out of habit. The minimal media coverage of the event made no mention of what Simon actually said.

This tract was written for anyone – politicians, the media, and the voting public – who are concerned about where we are as a nation, and who wants to know how we can improve.

How you make your decisions in the voting booth is up to you, but you should make sure to have enough accurate information to put the right people in office to do your bidding. Because as Thomas Jefferson said, "If a nation expects to be ignorant and free, in a state of civilization, it expects what never was and never will be."

Many issues face us today, and those people we elect should have at least an understanding of the bones of most issues; their thinking should be clear and their judgment sound. Of course, some people have a litmus test, but for the most part, you want to look at the whole person, the larger candidate, the person who will respond to issues that were discussed during the campaign; that is, how they think on their feet. So, even if a particular issue may not be important to us, how the matter is addressed could be illuminating.

Whomever we choose and for whatever reasons, those we elect should lead us to a society that best takes care of our children. Our forebears got that right. You may already know that our Constitution was built upon the Articles of Confederation, which were largely derived from the governing principles of the Iroquois, a confederacy comprised of six nations. When there was an issue to be resolved between two or more nations, the matriarch of each nation appointed a chief to figure it out. They didn't negotiate the way we do today. It wasn't, "You can fish in my stream if I can hunt in your forest." Instead, they resolved matters according to a single guideline: Whatever they decided had to benefit the sixth succeeding generation.

If we found the right leaders – bright, compassionate, practical people – then we could resolve some of the problems that have been mired in partisan politics for the past forty years according to such a demanding but empirical criterion, and we could then move toward a more optimistic future.

When this book was originally published in the late summer of 2006, it included several dozen questions for candidates that were relevant to the time. Most of those questions might be relevant today, because so little has been accomplished in Washington in the interim. In this revised edition, those questions have been left out. (If you are desperate, they are on the book's website, at TonySeton.com/TQI.)

Emblematic of this simplified edition of *The Quality Interview* is a simplified approach to questioning candidates. One might start by discussing the five most important issues the electorate wants resolved. These issues might vary from district to district and state by state, so we'll leave their selection to the local reporters. But then each issue can be examined simply on the basis of four questions:

What is an accurate description – the truth – about the current situation?

How did we get into the situation?

What is the best resolution?

How do we get there from here?

While one could spend hours discussing any important issue, both a politician and a journalist should be able to parse the essence of each issue in a matter of a few minutes. You could write down some critical notes on a topic and find that it wouldn't take very long to enumerate the critical points of each. I would humbly suggest that anyone running for Congress should be able to make clear his views on the five important subjects in less than fifteen minutes, and that would be generous.

But certainly any American serious about his country would willingly accord a quarter hour to determining the viability of a candidate. And let us note that it wouldn't require the whole interview, by any means, to produce a thumbs-up or down on someone. Most everyone would be listening for something new that made sense.

And let us not be swayed by the potential of such an approach to think that it might be quickly accomplished. First we have to persuade the American people that they can, as well as must, take back our country from the special interests who have led us down this path of corruption and failure. Consider that we have had troops in Iraq for no good reason for most of the past decade, and yet two-thirds of our young people, the younger electorate, couldn't find Iraq on a world map.

*   *   *   *   *   *

As noted above, some politicians don't know how to answer questions directly, so it is up to the interviewer to determine if they are being deliberately deceptive, incompetent, or if they simply misunderstood the question. Clarification should be pursued in a professional and non-hostile manner at all times; whether one is a reporter or a voter. If the politicians are being evasive or manipulative, or just trying to hide their ignorance, it will come across most clearly when the questioner maintains a calm, non-aggressive attitude.

By the same token, it is important that the interviewer persists to get either an answer, or a refusal to answer. One technique is to rephrase the question by saying something like, "I don't pay that much attention to the budget negotiations. Perhaps you can explain why you don't think that increasing the national debt is so important," or, "There are many people in this district who have relatives or friends who are stationed in Afghanistan. Don't you think they deserve to know the truth about how and why we got in and when and how we'll get out?"

Other, less pointed follow-ups, could be, "Let me ask the question this way," or "I don't think I asked that clearly," or "Let me tell you what I think our listeners want to know," or "That's not exactly what I meant." You get the idea. Candidates – all public figures, for that matter – have an obligation to answer questions so long as the answers sought aren't classified, or personal beyond the public's right to know.

The interviewer needs to extract an answer that will provide the readers/listeners with the information they need to understand both the issue and the candidate's position. Elicit from the candidate his thoughts on the appropriate directions and alternatives. His thinking, especially thinking out loud, can mean the difference between whether or not he should be sent to Congress.

To determine the best people to lead our country, citizens can easily check out the incumbents on the basis of their voting record. There are a number of non-partisan websites that do an excellent job of listing the critical issues that have been voted on by the Congress, and such information will provide a valuable basis for determining the mindset and effectiveness of the people already in office. Vote-smart.org and citizen.org are just two of such sites that list key votes. Choose your topic and see how your representative voted.

And in a broader sense, beyond the specifics of an individual's voting record, you might simply ask what progress has been made on virtually any issue since they've been in office. After all, they were elected the last time to deal with the nation's problems. What success have they had? Of course, each is only one of many voting members of Congress, but if a congress-man has been supping at the public trough for ten terms while education, health care, national security and the environment have all deteriorated, then maybe the voters should look to someone else to manage the nation's affairs.

Unfortunately, all too many interviews that go beyond the sound-bite level will elicit hems and haws and lots of shoulder-shrugging. A good direction then to take is to ask about the subjects of the committees on which the incumbent sits. What's been done to improve the situations you've been studying, Congressman? Why aren't we making more progress toward resolving these problems, Congressman? What are you doing to earn bipartisan support for a practical solution, Congressman? Why should you be sent back to Washington?

Inspiration

Covering the news can be a tremendously rewarding profession, when it is done right. Many of the people with whom I worked at ABC in the Seventies shared the sense of public service; that we were following a calling rather than just doing a job. Those who were so inspired always carried with them a small tape recorder and often a (film) camera. Hey, you never know. To wit....

In 1978, I was put in charge of the six-person unit that produced Barbara Walters' news appearances. This was a bone thrown to her, since she had been dumped as co-anchor. Because the climate was so hostile after her anchoring failed, my assignment and duties were often more political than journalistic. It was a no-win situation that stayed ugly because Barbara and the news executives refused to be honest with each other.

I went to Bonn for the 1978 G-7 Economic Summit as Barbara Walters' news producer. I hadn't been expecting to take the trip, since I'd been working on news stories in San Juan, St. Louis, Washington, and New York the week before.

So I found myself flying to London with Barbara and her researcher on the first leg of our trip to the German capital. In the first four days there, we did two interviews with German Chancellor Helmut Schmidt – one for the *World News Tonight* and the other for *Issues and Answers* (the ABC Sunday talk show later replaced by *This Week*) – in addition to several "flavor" pieces.

With nothing planned on the last day of the summit, Barbara and I happened to be walking through the ABC office when we heard a squawk on the walkie-talkie that someone named "Owens" needed a ride to the Palais Schaumberg, the site of the talks.

"That's Henry Owens!" Barbara said, recognizing the name of the official U.S. Ambassador to the Summit. "We'll take him!"

We ran out of the building, found Owens, and pushed him unceremoniously into Barbara's limousine. We tried our best to act nonchalant as Owens showed his credentials at the security checkpoint, and we continued into the Palais grounds.

We were the only journalists there, other than ZDF, the German television network. They had two studio cameras in position outside the Palais to provide live coverage of the heads of state leaving the final session.

Not wanting to be recognized and thrown out, Barbara and I shuffled unobtrusively about the grounds, staying near the fringes of the groups of aides and security people milling near the entrance of the Palais. After two hours, the aides stopped their milling and looked up expectantly. Jody Powell, President Carter's press secretary, recognized Barbara and walked over to us.

He seemed bemused and unconcerned with our presence.

Barbara asked if it would be possible to have a word with the President as he was leaving. Powell said he thought it would be possible, just as long as we didn't hold up the proceedings.

In a few minutes, the heads of state began to leave. Suddenly, I looked up and there was President Carter, standing just feet away, almost unnoticed. We quickly made our way over to him, inconspicuously taking out our micro-cassette recorders.

Standing behind Barbara and the President, I put a hand on each of their backs and gently shifted them so that they were facing the nearest ZDF camera.

The interview was brief, with the President stating his satisfaction with the way the talks had gone; and then it was over. Barbara got into one of the Carter staff cars, which would take her to the closing ceremonies. I took Barbara's car and driver and rushed back to the press headquarters. By walkie-talkie, I told senior ABC producer, Bob Siegenthaler, what had happened, and asked him to get a copy of the ZDF television coverage.

When I got back to the editing facility, it was a simple matter of hooking a few cables between the micro-cassette recorder and the videotape editing machine, and in minutes the synching of the interview – audio from micro-cassette, video from German television – was complete.

It was only a thirty-seven-second interview, and hardly earth-shattering. However, John Chancellor had interviewed Carter that morning, and it was supposed to have been the last exclusive from the talks. We went on air with our quick sound bite that said everything most viewers would care about, while NBC spent several minutes covering the same facts.

It was an extraordinary time, some of the most exciting weeks in my life. I did some of my best work in challenging circumstances. Most of it wasn't even on my radar before it arrived, but all was engaging and exhilarating. You don't make opportunities like that; you just make yourself ready to take advantage of them.

Other Books from Tony Seton

My principal activity over the past year or so has been the writing, editing, and publishing of books. A half-dozen in the past year. They include fiction and non-fiction and a new hybrid I call non-non-fiction. These are based on real events and/or circumstances and are designed to engage the reader and – he said humbly – to move us all forward in our thinking. Among the recent titles are:

Mayhem is a contemporary novel set in Marin County, California based on the mythic struggle between good and evil, with the author being called in to tip the tide of the titanic battle.

The Autobiography of John Dough, Gigolo is a novel about a former hedge fund manager who decides on a new path – to improve the lives of women. His clients include widows, divorcees and a gangster's moll.

Silver Lining is a novel about a shooting on the street that brings reporter David Skye and nurse Lucy Balfour together, for what becomes excitement and romance.

The Omega Crystal is a page-turner of a novel about how the petro industry is sitting on crucial developments in solar power capture and storage, waiting until their inventories run dry. Anchorman Geoff Lance uncovers the truth with the help – and love from – Ariane Chevasse, the beautiful and brilliant daughter of the inventor of The Omega Crystal.

Truth Be Told is a novelized version of a true story about an historic civil rights case of sexual harassment against a top-50 American law school.

From Terror to Triumph / The Herma Smith Curtis Story A true story of a young girl's survival of the Nazi occupation of Austria and her creation of a successful new life on the Monterey Peninsula.

Vision for a Healthy California is a road map for the Golden State. Written by Bill Monning, the highly-esteemed member of the California Assembly.

Three Lives of a Warrior is the stunning memoir of Phil Butler, who spent eight years as a prisoner of the North Vietnamese and came home to a new life.

The Power of the I AM by Dan Shafer is a breakthrough in self-awareness, and puts the power of meditation within reach of millions of people.

If you are interested in these books, or in having your own book written, edited and or published, please go online to TonySeton.com.